WHAT KiND OF QUiZ BOOK ARE YOU?

WHAT KiND OF QUiZ BOOK ARE YOU?

Pick Your Favorite Foods,
Characters & Celebrities
to Reveal Secrets
About Yourself

RACHEL McMAHON

ATRIA PAPERBACK

NEW YORK · LONDON · TORONTO · SYDNEY · NEW DELHI

ATRIA
PAPERBACK

An Imprint of Simon & Schuster, Inc.
1230 Avenue of the Americas
New York, NY 10020

Copyright © 2019 by Rachel McMahon

First Atria Paperback edition July 2019

ATRIA PAPERBACK and colophon are trademarks of Simon & Schuster, Inc.

For information about special discounts for bulk purchases,
please contact Simon & Schuster Special Sales at 1-866-506-1949
or business@simonandschuster.com.

The Simon & Schuster Speakers Bureau can bring authors
to your live event. For more information or to book an event,
contact the Simon & Schuster Speakers Bureau at 1-866-248-3049
or visit our website at www.simonspeakers.com.

Interior design by Dana Sloan

Manufactured in the United States of America

5 7 9 10 8 6 4

Library of Congress Cataloging-in-Publication Data has been applied for.

ISBN 978-1-9821-3249-1
ISBN 978-1-9821-3250-7 (ebook)

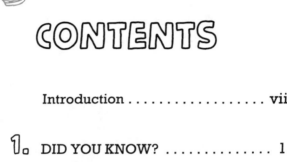

CONTENTS

INTRODUCTION

I'VE ALWAYS ENJOYED taking personality quizzes, from Which Celebrity Will You Marry? to Which Cupcake Flavor Are You?, and in high school I started playing around with creating them. The first ones were really just to make my friends laugh, but as I got better, I began submitting them to BuzzFeed.

When I left for college, I continued sending quizzes to BuzzFeed, and I could tell they were getting popular since the site often promoted them, and then Nick Jonas actually took my "Which Jonas Brother Are You?" quiz on Jimmy Fallon's show. And let me tell you, if you've spent your whole life in a small town in Michigan, it is a pretty wild moment to see something you've made on national television!

But that was only the beginning of the weirdness. After BuzzFeed's director of quizzes was let go as part of a big company layoff, he revealed in a blog post that I had actually created many of the site's most popular quizzes. I learned a couple of other things from his post, too: not only that this hobby of mine was a creative outlet that had racked up more than 135 million views in 2018 alone and was at times the second-largest traffic driver worldwide, but that there was also a human cost of a site relying on that much freely created content, as many employees ended up being let go. I have mixed feelings about BuzzFeed using its community to source unpaid content, but it was a great environment for me to learn and evolve in as a quiz maker. And I'm excited to continue to create them and share them in this new book.

The quizzes are as much for me as they are for you. I want them to be fun, and I look for inspiration in everyday life and what's tracking on social media. When I see lots of people talking about a show, movie, or celebrity, I make a quiz about it. Or if I see something when I'm walking around campus or town, such as a new ice cream shop or display of chips or Pop-Tarts, I write all the different types down for a later quiz.

I never take the quizzes too seriously. They are meant to be a little crazy and silly, but if they get you thinking about what is important to you and what you really want from life, that's great, too.

I hope you enjoy reading this book as much as I enjoyed writing it. If you want to know which state you belong in based on the food you choose or which kind of French fries you are, let's get started!

1

Did You Know?

Based on Your Favorite Things, Which Hair Color Should You Have?

1. Which of these is your favorite breakfast food?

a. Yogurt and fruit

b. Waffles

c. Eggs

d. Cereal

2. Which of these is your favorite color?

a. Yellow

b. Green

c. Orange

d. Black

3. Which of these is your favorite movie genre?

a. Romance

b. Comedy

c. Family-friendly

d. Action

4. Which of these is your favorite domestic animal?

a. Cat

b. Bunny

c. Horse

d. Dog

Continued

5. Which of these is your favorite dessert?

a. Chocolate mousse

b. Ice cream sandwich

c. Vanilla cupcake

d. Peanut butter cookie

6. Which of these is your favorite kind of YouTube video?

a. Makeup tutorial

b. Vlog

c. Reaction video

d. Comedy skit

7. Which of these is your favorite clothing item?

a. Dress/skirt

b. Leggings

c. Long-sleeved T-shirt

d. Sweatpants

8. Which of these is your favorite accessory?

a. Necklace

b. Bracelet

c. Earrings

d. Hat

9. Which of these is your favorite sport to watch?

a. Gymnastics

b. Snowboarding

c. Baseball

d. Basketball

10. Which of these is your favorite social media platform?

a. Facebook

b. Twitter

c. Pinterest

d. Instagram

11. Which of these is your favorite mythical creature?

a. Unicorn

b. Mermaid

c. Genie

d. Dragon

• •

If you picked mostly As—you got Platinum.

If you picked mostly Bs—you got Blue.

If you picked mostly Cs—you got Red.

If you picked mostly Ds—you got Gray.

Choose Some Movies to Reveal What People Love About You

1. Choose an action movie:
a. *The Fast and the Furious*

b. *Avengers: Infinity War*

c. *The Terminator*

d. *Taken*

2. Choose a horror movie:
a. *The Conjuring*

b. *Paranormal Activity*

c. *It*

d. *The Shining*

3. Choose a romantic movie:
a. *The Notebook*

b. *Pretty Woman*

c. *Me Before You*

d. *Dirty Dancing*

4. Choose a Pixar movie:
a. *The Incredibles*

b. *Monsters, Inc.*

c. *Finding Nemo*

d. *Up*

5. Choose a Disney princess movie:
a. *Pocahontas*

b. *Aladdin*

c. *Beauty and the Beast*

d. *The Little Mermaid*

6. Choose a teen movie:

a. *Clueless*

b. *Mean Girls*

c. *A Cinderella Story*

d. *Sixteen Candles*

7. Choose a comedy:

a. *Anchorman: The Legend of Ron Burgundy*

b. *21 Jump Street*

c. *Bridesmaids*

d. *Ace Ventura: Pet Detective*

8. Choose a holiday movie:

a. *Home Alone*

b. *Elf*

c. *National Lampoon's Christmas Vacation*

d. *How the Grinch Stole Christmas*

• •

If you picked mostly As—you're a strong leader, and people really respect you.

If you picked mostly Bs—you're hilarious and can always make people laugh.

If you picked mostly Cs—you always look for the best in people, and that's really admirable.

If you picked mostly Ds—you're a hard worker, and everyone admires your work ethic.

Based on Your Opinion of These Celebrities, How Will You Become Famous?

1. How do you feel about Tom Hanks?

   a. Like

   b. Dislike

   c. Neutral

2. How do you feel about Justin Bieber?

   a. Like

   b. Dislike

   c. Neutral

3. How do you feel about Harrison Ford?

   a. Like

   b. Dislike

   c. Neutral

4. How do you feel about Donald Trump?

   a. Like

   b. Dislike

   c. Neutral

5. How do you feel about Jennifer Aniston?

   a. Like

   b. Dislike

   c. Neutral

6. How do you feel about Janet Jackson?

a. Like

b. Dislike

c. Neutral

7. How do you feel about Kim Kardashian?

a. Like

b. Dislike

c. Neutral

8. How do you feel about Jim Carrey?

a. Like

b. Dislike

c. Neutral

9. How do you feel about Taylor Swift?

a. Like

b. Dislike

c. Neutral

• •

If you picked mostly As—you'll become famous by saving someone's life.

If you picked mostly Bs—you'll become famous by directing a popular movie.

If you picked mostly Cs—you'll become famous on YouTube.

Based on the Food You Order from the Kids' Menu, What Should Your Name Be?

1. Pick an item from Chick-fil-A's kids' menu:
 a. Chicken nuggets
 b. Grilled chicken nuggets
 c. Chicken strips
 d. Waffle fries

2. Pick an item from McDonald's kids' menu:
 a. Cheeseburger
 b. Nuggets
 c. Hamburger
 d. Fries

3. Pick an item from Wendy's kids' menu:
 a. Chicken nuggets
 b. Chicken wrap
 c. Fries
 d. Hamburger

4. Pick an item from Olive Garden's kids' menu:
 a. Pasta with meat sauce
 b. Pasta with alfredo sauce
 c. Mini pizza
 d. Cheese ravioli

5. Pick an item from Arby's kids' menu:

a. Ham and cheese slider

b. Roast beef and cheese slider

c. Chicken tenders

d. Curly fries

6. Pick an item from IHOP's kids' menu:

a. French toast with Nutella

b. Grilled cheese

c. Smiley face pancake

d. Chicken and waffles

7. Pick an item from Panera Bread's kids' menu:

a. Macaroni and cheese

b. French onion soup

c. Grilled cheese

d. Turkey and cheese sandwich

• •

If you picked mostly As—you got Jordyn.

If you picked mostly Bs—you got Bailey.

If you picked mostly Cs—you got Carter.

If you picked mostly Ds—you got Frankie.

Tell Us Your Junk Food Preferences, and We'll Tell You a Secret About Yourself

1. Choose a junk food:

    a. Potato chips

    b. Pop-Tarts

    c. Cinnamon roll

    d. Hot dog

2. Choose a junk food:

    a. Cheetos

    b. Pizza

    c. Tater tots

    d. Doughnut hole

3. Choose a junk food:

    a. Hamburger

    b. Ice cream

    c. Cookie

    d. Bacon

4. Choose a junk food:

    a. Mozzarella sticks

    b. Chicken nuggets

    c. Churros

    d. Brownie

5. Choose a junk food:

a. Oreos

b. Cupcake

c. French fries

d. Nachos

6. Choose a junk food:

a. Cheesecake

b. Fried chicken

c. Pancakes

d. Doritos

7. Choose a junk food:

a. Muffin

b. Milkshake

c. Chocolate bar

d. Buttered popcorn

• •

If you picked mostly As—your secret is that you get jealous of people really easily.

If you picked mostly Bs—your secret is that you're bad at saving money.

If you picked mostly Cs—your secret is that you cave in to peer pressure a lot.

If you picked mostly Ds—your secret is that you have been feeling lonely lately.

If You Were a Member of *The Incredibles*, What Superpower Would You Have?

1. Choose a Pixar movie:

  a. *Up*

  b. *Inside Out*

  c. *A Bug's Life*

  d. *Finding Nemo*

2. Choose a Pixar character:

  a. WALL-E from *WALL-E*

  b. Mater from *Cars*

  c. Remy from *Ratatouille*

  d. Boo from *Monsters, Inc.*

3. Choose a Disney princess:

  a. Ariel

  b. Rapunzel

  c. Belle

  d. Cinderella

4. Choose a Disney TV show:

  a. *Hannah Montana*

  b. *The Suite Life of Zack & Cody*

  c. *Kim Possible*

  d. *That's So Raven*

5. Choose a movie theater snack:

a. Skittles

b. Slushie

c. Popcorn

d. Soft pretzel

6. Choose a color:

a. Purple

b. Orange

c. Red

d. Mint green

7. Choose a superhero:

a. Iron Man

b. Spider-Man

c. Superman

d. Wonder Woman

8. Choose some cartoon superheroes:

a. The Powerpuff Girls

b. Mermaid Man and Barnacle Boy

c. Justice League

d. Teen Titans

• •

If you picked mostly As—you got Violet's invisibility.

If you picked mostly Bs—you got Dash's superspeed.

If you picked Cs—you got Mr. Incredible's superstrength.

If you picked Ds—you got Elastigirl's flexibility.

Which Reality TV Star Would Be Your Enemy?

~~~~~~~~~~~~~~~~~~~~~~~~~~~~~~~~~~

1. Which of these is most important to you?

a. Family

b. Fame

c. Friends

d. Happiness

2. Pick a food:

a. Avocado toast

b. Chicken nuggets

c. Hot dog

d. Sushi

3. Pick a job:

a. Writer

b. Lawyer

c. Doctor

d. Schoolteacher

4. Where would you like to spend the weekend?

a. At an amusement park

b. In the car on a road trip

d. In the mountains

d. At the beach

5. Pick a charity:

a. Salvation Army

b. St. Jude Children's Research Hospital

c. Red Cross

d. Boys & Girls Clubs of America

6. Pick an activity:

a. Reading

b. Working out

c. Drawing

d. Dancing

7. Pick a talk-show host:

a. Jimmy Kimmel

b. Conan O'Brien

c. Steve Harvey

d. Ellen DeGeneres

• •

If you picked mostly As—you got Abby Lee Miller from *Dance Moms*.

If you picked mostly Bs—you got Todd Chrisley from *Chrisley Knows Best*.

If you picked mostly Cs—you got Kim Kardashian from *Keeping Up with the Kardashians*.

If you picked mostly Ds—you got Donald Trump from *The Celebrity Apprentice*.

Based on the Foods You Select, What Is Your Mental Age?

1. Choose a Chinese food:

    a. Szechuan chicken

    b. Fried mashi

    c. Spring rolls

    d. Dumplings

2. Choose an Italian food:

    a. Caprese salad

    b. Pasta carbonara

    c. Bruschetta

    d. Tiramisù

3. Choose an American food:

    a. Meat loaf

    b. Pecan pie

    c. Tater tots

    d. Corn dog

4. Choose a Mexican food:

    a. Gorditas

    b. Tamales

    c. Enchiladas

    d. Tacos

5. Choose an Indian food:

a. Biryani

b. Tandoori chicken

c. Samosa

d. Naan

6. Choose a Caribbean food:

a. Conch chowder

b. Jerk chicken

c. Pineapple chow

d. Macaroni pie

7. Choose a Mediterranean food:

a. Tagine

b. Couscous salad

c. Gyro

d. Hummus

8. Choose a Japanese food:

a. Tempura

b. Sukiyaki

c. Sushi

d. Beef udon

• •

If you picked mostly As—you got 45 years old.

If you picked mostly Bs—you got 28 years old.

If you picked mostly Cs—you got 19 years old.

If you picked mostly Ds—you got 10 years old.

What Magazine Cover Do You Belong On?

1. How old are you?

a. Under 20 years old

b. 20 to 29 years old

c. 30 to 39 years old

d. 40 years old and up

2. Choose a word to describe yourself:

a. Youthful

b. Stylish

c. Caring

d. Bright

3. Choose an appetizer:

a. Boneless wings

b. Pita bread

c. Caprese salad

d. Bruschetta

4. Choose a game to play:

a. The Game of Life

b. Cards Against Humanity

c. Charades

d. Bingo

5. Choose a piece of clothing:

a. Shoes

b. Hoodie

c. Dress

d. Socks

6. Choose an accessory:

a. Bracelet

b. Sunglasses

c. Earrings

d. Necklace

7. Choose a female celebrity:

a. Ariana Grande

b. Cindy Crawford

c. Angelina Jolie

d. Meryl Streep

• •

If you picked mostly As—you got *Seventeen*.

If you picked mostly Bs—you got *Vogue*.

If you picked mostly Cs—you got *People*.

If you picked mostly Ds—you got *Time*.

Which Game Show Are You Destined to Be On?

1. Choose a board game:

　　a. The Game of Life

　　b. Monopoly

　　c. Risk

　　d. Pictionary

2. Choose a video game:

　　a. Mario Kart

　　b. Super Smash Bros.

　　c. Call of Duty

　　d. Fortnite

3. Choose a game app:

　　a. Words with Friends

　　b. Candy Crush Saga

　　c. Angry Birds

　　d. Cut the Rope

4. Choose a word to describe yourself:

　　a. Fun

　　b. Determined

　　c. Daring

　　d. Logical

5. Choose the most important thing to you:

a. Family

b. Intelligence

c. Life experiences

d. Money

6. Choose a TV network:

a. CBS

b. NBC

c. FOX

d. ABC

• •

If you picked mostly **As**—you got *Family Feud*.

If you picked mostly **Bs**—you got *Wheel of Fortune*.

If you picked mostly **Cs**—you got *Deal or No Deal*.

If you picked mostly **Ds**—you got *The Price Is Right*.

Based on the Bucket List You Make, Which Shade of Blue Are You?

1. Add something to your bucket list:

    a. Write a book

    b. Win a hot dog–eating contest

    c. See the northern lights (aurora borealis)

2. Add something to your bucket list:

    a. Learn to bake

    b. See the pyramids in Egypt

    c. Volunteer with elephants

3. Add something to your bucket list:

    a. Learn to surf

    b. Go skydiving

    c. Do goat yoga

4. Add something to your bucket list:

    a. Visit Hawaii

    b. Bungee jump

    c. Go to Disney World

5. Add something to your bucket list:

    a. Learn to play guitar

    b. Swim with sharks

    c. Visit the Eiffel Tower

6. Add something to your bucket list:

   a. Visit New York City

   b. Ride in a hot air balloon

   c. Adopt a dog

7. Add something to your bucket list:

   a. Go on an Alaskan cruise

   b. Run a marathon

   c. Learn a new language

8. Add something to your bucket list:

   a. Go scuba diving

   b. Ride a camel

   c. Hold a baby panda

• •

If you picked mostly As—you got Turquoise.

   • You're energetic and full of passion.

If you picked mostly Bs—you got Navy Blue.

   • You're strong-willed and confident.

If you picked mostly Cs—you got Baby Blue.

   • You're a soft and caring person.

What Weird Place Should You Get Married At?

1. Choose a restaurant:

   a. Subway

   b. Pizza Hut

   c. Outback Steakhouse

   d. Denny's

2. Choose a celebrity couple:

   a. Ashton Kutcher and Mila Kunis

   b. Will Smith and Jada Pinkett Smith

   c. Barack and Michelle Obama

   d. Ryan Reynolds and Blake Lively

3. What age would you want to stay forever?

   a. 16 years old

   b. 8 years old

   c. 26 years old

   d. 21 years old

4. Which of these gross food combinations would you try?

   a. Chocolate chip cookies and ranch dressing

   b. Hot dogs and applesauce

   c. Ketchup on white rice

   d. Strawberry jam and sour cream

5. Which pattern is your favorite?

a. Polka dots

b. Tie-dye

c. Stripes

d. Chevron

6. Which weird smell do you enjoy the most?

a. Chlorine

b. Sharpie marker

c. Gas

d. Leather seat

7. What color scheme would you want for your wedding:

a. Shades of purple

b. Turquoise

c. Gold and burgundy

d. Peach and light blue

• •

If you picked mostly As—you got Rainforest Cafe.

If you picked mostly Bs—you got Chuck E. Cheese's.

If you picked mostly Cs—you got Prison.

If you picked mostly Ds—you got Doughnut Shop.

Create Your Own Quiz, and We'll Reveal One of Your Dominant Personality Traits

1. What is going to be the title of your quiz?

    a. "Which powerful woman are you?"

    b. "Answer these questions, and we'll give you something to put on your bucket list."

    c. "What kind of partygoer are you?"

2. How many possible results is your quiz going to have?

    a. 4

    b. 6

    c. As many as possible

3. How many questions is your quiz going to have?

    a. 6

    b. 10

    c. 15 or more

4. Will your quiz include pictures?

    a. No, just text

    b. Some pictures and some text

    c. Yes, lots of pictures!

5. Which of these would be a question on your quiz?

    a. "What is something that is important to you?"

    b. "What's something you've always wanted to try?"

    c. "How would your friends describe you?"

● ●

If you picked mostly As—you got Conscientiousness.

- You have a tendency to be careful, follow rules, work hard, and be on time.

If you picked mostly Bs—you got Openness.

- You have a tendency to appreciate new things.

If you picked mostly Cs—you got Extroversion.

- You have a tendency to be talkative and social, with a style of your own.

Pick Some Warm Foods, and We'll Reveal Which Cold Food You Are Most Like

1. Pick a warm food:

    a. Quesadilla

    b. Chili

    c. Sausage

2. Pick a warm food:

    a. Buffalo wings

    b. Scrambled eggs

    c. Beef stew

3. Pick a warm food:

    a. Steak

    b. Hot cheese dip

    c. Baked potato

4. Pick a warm food:

    a. Pizza

    b. Hot ham and cheese sandwich

    c. Corn

5. Pick a warm food:

    a. French fries

    b. Chicken noodle soup

    c. Apple crisp

6. Pick a warm food:

a. Mozzarella sticks

b. Stir-fry

c. Baked beans

7. Pick a warm food:

a. Spicy chicken nuggets

b. Macaroni and cheese

c. Hot oatmeal

• •

If you picked mostly As—you got Ice Cream.

• You're fun.

If you picked mostly Bs—you got Pasta Salad.

• You're bold.

If you picked mostly Cs—you got Frozen Blueberries.

• You're classic.

Based on the Stack of Pancakes You'd Build, What Word Best Describes You?

1. Choose the first pancake for your stack:

a. Buttermilk pancake

b. Cinnamon roll pancake

c. Salted caramel pancake

2. Choose the second pancake:

a. Chocolate chip pancake

b. Pumpkin pancake

c. New York cheesecake pancake

3. Choose the third pancake:

a. Blueberry pancake

b. Strawberry banana pancake

c. Red velvet pancake

4. Choose the fourth pancake:

a. Buttermilk pancake

b. Dark chocolate pancake

c. Funfetti pancake

5. Choose a topping:

a. Butter

b. Whipped cream

c. Scoop of ice cream

6. Choose another topping:

a. Syrup

b. Peanut butter

c. Sprinkles

• •

If you picked mostly As—you got Predictable.

If you picked mostly Bs—you got Considerate.

If you picked mostly Cs—you got Easygoing.

2

Guess What?

Based on Whether or Not You Think These Things Are Overrated, We Know If You're a Millennial or Not

1. **Ed Sheeran is:**
   a. Overrated
   b. Not overrated

2. **Beyoncé is:**
   a. Overrated
   b. Not overrated

3. **The TV show *Stranger Things* is:**
   a. Overrated
   b. Not overrated

4. **The movie *The Notebook* is:**
   a. Overrated
   b. Not overrated

5. **Pizza is:**
   a. Overrated
   b. Not overrated

6. **Brunch is:**
   a. Overrated
   b. Not overrated

Continued

7. Good looks are:

a. Overrated

b. Not overrated

8. The fast-food restaurant Chick-fil-A is:

a. Overrated

b. Not overrated

9. The reality TV show *The Bachelor* is:

a. Overrated

b. Not overrated

10. Avocados are:

a. Overrated

b. Not overrated

11. The sound of rain is:

a. Overrated

b. Not overrated

12. British accents are:

a. Overrated

b. Not overrated

13. Chocolate is:

a. Overrated

b. Not overrated

14. Going to the beach is:

a. Overrated

b. Not overrated

15. Social media are:

a. Overrated

b. Not overrated

16. Yoga is:

a. Overrated

b. Not overrated

17. The movie series *Harry Potter* is:

a. Overrated

b. Not overrated

18. Starbucks is:

a. Overrated

b. Not overrated

• •

If you picked mostly As—you are not a millennial.

If you picked mostly Bs—you are a millennial.

ick Some Weird Food Combos, and We'll Tell You If You Are an Introvert or an Extrovert

1. Choose a weird food combination:

a. Peanut butter and cheese

b. Pickle and peanut butter sandwich

2. Choose a weird food combination:

a. Salt and pepper on apples

b. Hot dogs and SpaghettiOs

3. Choose a weird food combination:

a. Jelly on scrambled eggs

b. Peanut butter and jelly hot dog

4. Choose a weird food combination:

a. Ketchup on rice

b. Ketchup on macaroni and cheese

5. Choose a weird food combination:

a. Chips in a sandwich

b. Chocolate on potato chips

6. Choose a weird food combination:

a. Bread with butter and sugar

b. Cheetos in milk

7. Choose a weird food combination:

a. Soy sauce on ice cream

b. French fries and ice cream

8. Choose a weird food combination:

a. Tomato sauce on pancakes

b. Ranch on pancakes

9. Choose a weird food combination:

a. Spaghetti sandwich

b. Spaghetti taco

10. Choose a weird food combination:

a. Grapes and salami

b. Bacon and chocolate

• •

If you picked mostly As—you got Introvert.

- You tend to recharge by spending time alone. Normally, you lose energy from being around people for long periods of time, particularly large crowds.

If you picked mostly Bs—you got Extrovert.

- You tend to gain energy from other people. You find that your energy decreases when you spend too much time alone, and you're recharged by being social.

Based on Your Choices, We'll Guess If You Prefer Chocolate or Vanilla

~~~~~~

1. Are you a morning person or a night person?

  a. Morning person

  b. Night person

2. Do you prefer board games or video games?

  a. Board games

  b. Video games

3. Do you prefer salty or sweet foods?

  a. Salty foods

  b. Sweet foods

4. Do you prefer smoothies or milkshakes?

  a. Smoothies

  b. Milkshakes

5. Do you prefer Facebook or Instagram?

  a. Facebook

  b. Instagram

6. Do you prefer red or blue?

  a. Red

  b. Blue

7. Do you prefer apples or bananas?

   a. Apples

   b. Bananas

8. Do you prefer using a pencil or a pen?

   a. A pencil

   b. A pen

9. Do you normally prefer the book or the movie?

   a. The book

   b. The movie

10. Do you prefer texting or calling?

   a. Texting

   b. Calling

• •

If you picked mostly As—you got Vanilla.

If you picked mostly Bs—you got Chocolate.

Based on the Colors You Choose, We'll Guess Your Current Mood

1. Choose a color that reminds you of the word *sweet*:

   a. Purple

   b. Pink

   c. Red

2. Choose a color that reminds you of the word *hate*:

   a. Dark red

   b. Orange

   c. Black

3. Choose a color that reminds you of the word *success*:

   a. Gold

   b. Green

   c. Yellow

4. Choose a color that reminds you of the word *news*:

   a. Yellow

   b. Blue

   c. White

5. Choose a color that reminds you of the word *family*:

   a. Green

   b. Red

   c. Blue

6. Choose a color that reminds you of the word *healthy*:

    a. Light pink

    b. Red

    c. Brown

7. Choose a color that reminds you of the word *career*:

    a. Purple

    b. Orange

    c. Green

• •

If you picked mostly As—you got Relaxed.

If you picked mostly Bs—you got Giddy.

If you picked mostly Cs—you got Irritated.

Based on the Appetizers You Pick, We'll Guess Your Zodiac Sign

1. Pick an appetizer:

  a. Potato skins

  b. Bacon cheddar tots

  c. Caprese salad skewers

  d. Mozzarella sticks

2. Pick an appetizer:

  a. Quesadilla

  b. Spinach and artichoke dip

  c. Ham and cheese roll-ups

  d. Garlic bread

3. Pick an appetizer:

  a. Cheese and crackers

  b. French fries

  c. Fried pickles

  d. Mini stuffed peppers

4. Pick an appetizer:

  a. Rolls

  b. Onion rings

  c. Egg rolls

  d. Nachos

5. Pick an appetizer:

a. Mini taco cups

b. Pigs in a blanket

c. Salami and cream cheese bites

d. Chips and salsa

6. Pick an appetizer:

a. Bacon pineapple bites

b. Deviled eggs

c. Crockpot sausages

d. Chips and guacamole

7. Pick an appetizer:

a. Cheese fries

b. Pretzel bites

c. Barbecue meatballs

d. Bacon-wrapped brown sugar smokies

• •

If you picked mostly As—you got Gemini, Libra, or Aquarius.

If you picked mostly Bs—you got Taurus, Virgo, or Capricorn.

If you picked mostly Cs—you got Cancer, Scorpio, or Pisces.

If you picked mostly Ds—you got Aries, Leo, or Sagittarius.

Based on Your Food Preferences, We'll Guess If You're a Morning Person or a Night Person

1. **Would you rather get free french fries for a year or free breadsticks for a year?**

   a. French fries

   b. Breadsticks

2. **Would you rather eat an entire pizza or an entire cake by yourself?**

   a. Pizza

   b. Cake

3. **Would you rather get a free tub of ice cream or a free tub of mashed potatoes?**

   a. Ice cream

   b. Mashed potatoes

4. **Would you rather never eat chocolate again or never eat fruit candy again?**

   a. Chocolate

   b. Fruit candy

5. **Would you rather have a dessert or a sandwich named after you?**

   a. Dessert

   b. Sandwich

6. Would you rather eat hamburger or macaroni and cheese for breakfast?

   a. Hamburger

   b. Macaroni and cheese

7. Would you rather eat only hot dog buns or only plain pasta for a week straight?

   a. Hot dog buns

   b. Plain pasta

8. Would you rather have a taco or an ice cream taco?

   a. Taco

   b. Ice cream taco

• •

If you picked mostly As—you got Night.

If you picked mostly Bs—you got Morning.

Eat Some Food in Every Color, and We'll Guess Your Biggest Pet Peeve

1. Eat a red food:

   a. Apple

   b. Pepperoni

   c. Cherries

2. Eat an orange food:

   a. Carrots

   b. Cheddar cheese

   c. Sweet potato

3. Eat a yellow food:

   a. Corn

   b. Lemon meringue pie

   c. Banana

4. Eat a green food:

   a. Green beans

   b. Guacamole

   c. Cucumber

5. Eat a blue food:

   a. Blueberries

   b. Cotton candy

   c. Blue corn chips

6. Eat a purple food:

a. Grapes

b. Wildlicious Wild! Berry Pop-Tarts

c. Plums

7. Eat a pink food:

a. Raspberries

b. Strawberry ice cream

c. Ham

8. Eat a white food:

a. Rice

b. Ranch dressing

c. Marshmallows

• •

If you picked mostly As—you got Bad Grammar.

If you picked mostly Bs—you got Slow Walkers/Drivers.

If you picked mostly Cs—you got Rude People.

Based on the Weird Ice Cream Flavors You Pick, We'll Guess If You Prefer Fruits or Vegetables

1. Pick a weird ice cream flavor:

    a. Buttered toast ice cream

    b. Fried chicken ice cream

2. Pick a weird ice cream flavor:

    a. Pizza ice cream

    b. Garlic bread ice cream

3. Pick a weird ice cream flavor:

    a. Bacon ice cream

    b. Parmesan cheese ice cream

4. Pick a weird ice cream flavor:

    a. Taco ice cream

    b. Baked bean ice cream

5. Pick a weird ice cream flavor:

    a. Froot Loops ice cream

    b. Hot Cheetos ice cream

6. Pick a weird ice cream flavor:

    a. Hummus ice cream

    b. Meatball ice cream

7. Pick a weird ice cream flavor:

    a. Fish-and-chips ice cream

    b. Jalapeño ice cream

8. Pick a weird ice cream flavor:

    a. Sushi ice cream

    b. Chicken noodle soup ice cream

9. Pick a weird ice cream flavor

    a. Candy corn ice cream

    b. Doritos ice cream

10. Pick a weird ice cream flavor:

    a. Avocado ice cream

    b. Sweet corn ice cream

• •

If you picked mostly As—you got Fruits.

If you picked mostly Bs—you got Vegetables.

Like or Pass on These Flavors of Pop-Tarts, and We'll Guess Your Relationship Status

1. Brown Sugar Cinnamon:
   a. Like
   b. Pass

2. Cherry:
   a. Like
   b. Pass

3. Chocolate Fudge:
   a. Like
   b. Pass

4. Strawberry:
   a. Like
   b. Pass

5. Blueberry:
   a. Like
   b. Pass

6. Wildlicious Wild! Berry:
   a. Like
   b. Pass

7. Raspberry:

   a. Like

   b. Pass

8. Cookies & Creme:

   a. Like

   b. Pass

9. Confetti Cupcake:

   a. Like

   b. Pass

10. Chocolate Chip:

   a. Like

   b. Pass

11. Cinnamon Roll:

   a. Like

   b. Pass

12. S'mores:

   a. Like

   b. Pass

• •

If you picked mostly As—you got Single.

If you picked mostly Bs—you got Taken.

Based on What You Buy at the Grocery Store, We'll Guess Your Favorite TV Show Genre

1. Add something to your cart:

   a. Potato chips

   b. Pop-Tarts

   c. Chicken noodle soup

   d. Milk

   e. Apples

2. Add something to your cart:

   a. Popcorn

   b. Tater tots

   c. Peanut butter

   d. Go-Gurt yogurt

   e. Loaf of bread

3. Add something to your cart:

   a. Chex Mix

   b. Frosted Flakes

   c. Head of lettuce

   d. Cinnamon rolls

   e. Garlic bread

4. Add something to your cart:

   a. Grapes

   b. Frozen pizza

c. Rotisserie chicken

d. Frosted sugar cookies

e. Cheese sticks

5. Add something to your cart:

a. Frozen lasagna

b. Boxed macaroni and cheese

c. M&M's

d. Animal crackers

e. Canned corn

6. Add something to your cart:

a. Bagels

b. Hot dogs

c. Granola bar

d. Fruit snacks

e. Bananas

7. Add something to your cart:

a. Oreos

b. Cake mix

c. Tortillas

d. Pretzels

e. Pasta sauce

8. Add something to your cart:

a. Diet Coke

b. Ice cream

c. Blueberries

d. Peanuts

e. Potatoes   *Continued*

9. Add something to your cart:

a. Lemonade

b. Frozen waffles

c. Crackers

d. Mozzarella sticks

e. Doughnuts

• •

If you picked mostly As—you got Crime.

If you picked mostly Bs—you got Comedy.

If you picked mostly Cs—you got Sci-fi.

If you picked mostly Ds—you got Animated.

If you picked mostly Es—you got Action.

Based on Your Favorite Chips, We'll Guess If You Prefer Cats or Dogs

1. Cool Ranch Doritos or Nacho Cheese Doritos?

a. Cool Ranch Doritos

b. Nacho Cheese Doritos

2. Cheetos or Fritos?

a. Cheetos

b. Fritos

3. Veggie Straws or SunChips?

a. Veggie Straws

b. SunChips

4. Sour cream and onion chips or cheddar cheese chips?

a. Sour cream and onion chips

b. Cheddar cheese chips

5. Lay's Classic or Ruffles Original?

a. Lay's Classic

b. Ruffles Original

6. Pita chips or tortilla chips?

a. Pita chips

b. Tortilla chips

If you got mostly **As**—you got Cats.

If you got mostly **Bs**—you got Dogs.

Based on Your Favorite Sweets, We'll Guess If You Prefer M&M's or Skittles

1. Choose a sweet:
- a. Apple pie
- b. Red velvet cake

2. Choose a sweet:
- a. Strawberry ice cream
- b. Chocolate chip cookie

3. Choose a sweet:
- a. Crème brûlée
- b. Cheesecake

4. Choose a sweet:
- a. Peanut butter cookie
- b. Brownie

5. Choose a sweet:
- a. Banana split
- b. S'mores

6. Choose a sweet:
- a. Cinnamon roll
- b. Doughnut

7. Choose a sweet:

  a. Blondie

  b. Tiramisù

8. Choose a sweet:

  a. Sugar cookie

  b. Churros

9. Choose a sweet:

  a. Caramel apple

  b. Fudge

10. Choose a sweet:

  a. Sherbet

  b. Cannoli

• •

If you picked mostly As—you got Skittles.

If you picked mostly Bs—you got M&M's.

Based on the Summer Activities You Choose, We'll Guess Your Age

1. Choose a summer activity:

    a. Swimming

    b. Going to an outdoor concert

    c. Camping

    d. Stargazing

2. Choose a summer activity:

    a. Going to a waterpark

    b. Tubing

    c. Going mini golfing

    d. Having a picnic

3. Choose a summer activity:

    a. Going to an amusement park

    b. Wakeboarding

    c. Riding a bike

    d. Having a barbecue

4. Choose a summer activity:

    a. Tie-dyeing

    b. Wake surfing

    c. Snorkeling

    d. Going to the beach

5. Choose a summer activity:

    a. Going to a fair

    b. Lying out in the sun

c. Playing volleyball

d. Kayaking

6. Choose a summer activity:

a. Playing with sidewalk chalk

b. Jet skiing

c. Having a water balloon fight

d. Going to a drive-in movie

7. Choose a summer activity:

a. Eating ice cream

b. Waterskiing

c. Sitting around a campfire

d. Lounging in a hammock

8. Choose a summer activity:

a. Going to the zoo

b. Kneeboarding

c. Zip-lining

d. Paddleboarding

• •

If you picked mostly As—you got 15 years old or younger.

If you picked mostly Bs—you got 16 to 24 years old.

If you picked mostly Cs—you got 25 to 39 years old.

If you picked mostly Ds—you got 40 years or older.

Based on the Foods You Pick, We'll Guess If You Prefer Summer or Fall

1. Choose a food:
a. Mashed potatoes

b. Potato chips

2. Choose a food:
a. Green beans

b. Watermelon

3. Choose a food:
a. Macaroni and cheese

b. Potato salad

4. Choose a food:
a. Corn bread

b. Sandwiches

5. Choose a food:
a. Turkey

b. Hot dog

6. Choose a food:
a. Pie

b. Soft-serve ice cream

7. Choose a food:
a. Sweet corn

b. Baked beans

8. Choose a food:

a. Soup

b. Salad

9. Choose a food:

a. Pasta

b. Pizza

10. Choose a food:

a. Apple

b. Blueberries

• •

If you picked mostly As—you got Fall.

If you picked mostly Bs—you got Summer.

Reveal How You Feel about These Foods, and We Will Guess a Fear of Yours

1. How do you feel about deep-dish pizza?

a. Yuck

b. It's okay

c. Yum

2. How do you feel about peas?

a. Yuck

b. They're okay

c. Yum

3. How do you feel about chicken pot pie?

a. Yuck

b. It's okay

c. Yum

4. How do you feel about ice cream sandwiches?

a. Yuck

b. They're okay

c. Yum

5. How do you feel about hot dogs?

a. Yuck

b. They're okay

c. Yum

6. How do you feel about cheese popcorn?

a. Yuck

b. It's okay

c. Yum

7. How do you feel about onion rings?

a. Yuck

b. They're okay

c. Yum

8. How do you feel about sushi?

a. Yuck

b. It's okay

c. Yum

9. How do you feel about fried chicken?

a. Yuck

b. It's okay

c. Yum

10. How do you feel about blueberries?

a. Yuck

b. They're okay

c. Yum

• •

If you picked mostly As—you got Fear of Change.

If you picked mostly Bs—you got Fear of Commitment.

If you picked mostly Cs—you got Fear of Being Lonely.

Based on Your Favorite Ice Cream Flavors, We'll Guess Your Favorite Kind of Pizza

1. Which of these is your favorite ice cream flavor?

   a. Vanilla

   b. Strawberry

   c. Chocolate

2. Which of these is your favorite ice cream flavor?

   a. Butter pecan

   b. Pistachio

   c. Coffee

3. Which of these is your favorite ice cream flavor?

   a. Mint chocolate chip

   b. Birthday Cake

   c. Rocky Road

4. Which of these is your favorite ice cream flavor?

   a. Cookies and cream

   b. Peanut butter

   c. Chocolate chip cookie dough

5. Which of these is your favorite ice cream flavor?

   a. Cherry vanilla

   b. Mango

   c. Strawberry cheesecake

6. **Which of these is your favorite ice cream flavor?**

   a. Chocolate peanut butter

   b. Rainbow sherbet

   c. Cinnamon bun

7. **Which of these is your favorite ice cream flavor?**

   a. Blue moon

   b. Neapolitan

   c. Cotton candy

8. **Which of these is your favorite kind of ice cream sundae?**

   a. Caramel nut

   b. Strawberry

   c. Chocolate fudge

9. **Choose a crazy ice cream flavor:**

   a. Corn on the cob

   b. Sweet potato

   c. Cheetos

10. **Which of these is your favorite milkshake flavor?**

   a. Chocolate banana

   b. Orange creamsicle

   c. Oreo cheesecake

• •

If you picked mostly As—you got Thin-Crust Pizza.

If you picked mostly Bs—you got Neapolitan Pizza.

If you picked mostly Cs—you got Deep-Dish Pizza.

Based on the Pie Flavors You Choose, We'll Guess If You Are Creative or Not

1. Choose a pie flavor:
- a. Boston cream
- b. Key lime

2. Choose a pie flavor:
- a. Lemon meringue
- b. Blueberry

3. Choose a pie flavor:
- a. Chocolate silk
- b. Peach

4. Choose a pie flavor:
- a. Pumpkin
- b. Apple

5. Choose a pie flavor:
- a. Banana cream
- b. Coconut cream

6. Choose a pie flavor:
- a. Peanut butter
- b. Pecan

• •

If you picked mostly As—you got Very Creative.

If you picked mostly Bs—you got Not So Creative.

3

Find Your Match

Which Travel Destination Is Your Perfect Match?

1. Which of these is your favorite candy?

a. Tropical Skittles

b. Swedish Fish

c. Sour Patch Kids

d. Hershey's Kisses Milk Chocolate

e. Starbursts

f. Reese's Peanut Butter Cups

2. What is the perfect temperature for you?

a. 80 degrees or higher

b. 70 to 80 degrees

c. 55 degrees or lower

d. 65 to 70 degrees

e. 55 to 60 degrees

f. 60 to 65 degrees

3. Which of these is your favorite animal?

a. Sea turtle

b. Kangaroo

c. Dog

d. Dolphin

e. Bear

f. Seal

4. Which of these foods would you like to eat for breakfast?

a. Bowl of fresh fruit

b. Toast

c. Breakfast sandwich

d. Waffles

e. Eggs

f. Croissant

5. Which of these foods would you like to eat for lunch?

a. Salad

b. Fish and chips

c. Chicken nuggets and fries

d. Gyro

e. Macaroni and cheese

f. Pizza

6. Which of these foods would you like to eat for dinner?

a. Meat kabobs

b. Salmon

c. Steak and mashed potatoes

d. Chicken parmigiana

e. Ribs

f. Spaghetti

7. Which of the following activities seems most fun to you?

a. Relaxing on the beach

b. Going to an amusement park

c. Exploring a city

d. Going on a scenic bike tour

e. Hiking

f. Shopping

Continued

8. Which of these celebrities would you like to have join you on vacation?

a. Ariana Grande

b. Chris Pratt

c. Bruno Mars

d. Zendaya

e. Channing Tatum

f. Jennifer Lawrence

9. Which is your favorite social media platform?

a. Instagram

b. Snapchat

c. Facebook

d. Pinterest

e. Twitter

f. I don't like social media

10. Which of these desserts would you like to eat?

a. Strawberry shortcake

b. Churros

c. Blueberry pie

d. Cream puff

e. Ice cream sandwich

f. Tiramisù

11. Which of these is your favorite Disney cartoon character?

a. Minnie Mouse

b. Goofy

c. Daisy Duck

d. Donald Duck

e. Pluto

f. Mickey Mouse

• •

If you picked mostly As—you should travel to the Maldives.

If you picked mostly Bs—you should travel to Sydney.

If you picked mostly Cs—you should travel to New York City.

If you picked mostly Ds—you should travel to Santorini.

If you picked mostly Es—you should travel to Yosemite National Park.

If you picked mostly Fs—you should travel to Florence.

Which Movie Series Do You Belong In?

1. Choose a word to describe yourself:

  a. Daring

  b. Competitive

  c. Energetic

2. Choose a movie genre:

  a. Action

  b. Family-friendly

  c. Science fiction

3. Choose a movie snack:

  a. Soft pretzel

  b. Popcorn

  c. Candy

4. Choose an activity:

  a. Working out

  b. Swimming

  c. Reading

5. How daring are you?

  a. Very

  b. Not at all

  c. Somewhat

6. Choose a country:

   a. United States

   b. Ireland

   c. Japan

7. Choose an actor:

   a. Will Smith

   b. Leonardo DiCaprio

   c. Tom Cruise

8. Choose an actress:

   a. Jennifer Lawrence

   b. Julia Roberts

   c. Meryl Streep

• •

If you picked mostly As—you got the *Divergent* movie series.

- You're brave and determined; this movie series is your perfect fit.

If you picked mostly Bs—you got the *Harry Potter* movie series.

- You don't realize your own strength and power; starring in this movie series would be eye-opening for you.

If you picked mostly Cs—you got the *Star Wars* movie series.

- You may act 100 percent cool on the outside, but deep down you're a little nerdy and love going on adventures.

Build a Cake, and We'll Match You with a Lucky Number

1. Choose the flavor of the first tier:

    a. White chocolate raspberry

    b. Salted caramel

    c. Vanilla

    d. Pumpkin

2. Choose the flavor of the second tier:

    a. Sticky toffee

    b. Marble

    c. Chocolate

    d. Strawberry

3. Choose the flavor of the third tier:

    a. Lemon

    b. Funfetti

    c. Red velvet

    d. Pistachio

4. Choose a frosting:

    a. Cream cheese

    b. Chocolate ganache

    c. Buttercream

    d. No frosting

5. Choose a candy topping:

a. Reese's Pieces

b. Skittles

c. Milk chocolate M&M's

d. None, thanks

6. Choose another topping:

a. Whipped cream

b. Mini marshmallows

c. Sprinkles

d. Strawberries

• •

If you picked mostly As—you got 1.

If you picked mostly Bs—you got 19.

If you picked mostly Cs—you got 7.

If you picked mostly Ds—you got 23.

Based on the Desserts You Choose, Which Decade Do You Belong In?

1. Choose a dessert:
- a. Ice cream
- b. Ice cream cake
- c. Ice cream sandwich

2. Choose a dessert:
- a. Butterscotch blondie
- b. Fudge brownie
- c. Strawberry white chocolate brownie

3. Choose a dessert:
- a. Custard
- b. Pie
- c. Cheesecake

4. Choose a dessert:
- a. Milkshake
- b. Ice cream sundae
- c. Frozen yogurt

5. Choose a dessert:
- a. Sugar cookie
- b. Snickerdoodle cookie
- c. Chocolate chip cookie

6. Choose a dessert:

  a. Chocolate mousse

  b. Banana pudding

  c. Jell-O lasagna

7. Choose a dessert:

  a. Pound cake

  b. Bundt cake

  c. Coffee cake

8. Choose a dessert:

  a. Cherry pie

  b. Blueberry pie

  c. Apple pie

• •

If you picked mostly As—you got the 1920s.

  • You're the perfect fit for the exuberant, freewheeling popular culture of this decade.

If you picked mostly Bs—you got the 1970s.

  • You'd fit in nicely with this decade of social change.

If you picked mostly Cs—you got the 1990s.

  • You'd be a great fit for this awesome pop culture decade.

Based on the Salty Foods You Pick, Which Unique Job Should You Do?

1. Pick a salty food:

    a. Sweet potato chips

    b. Cheddar Goldfish crackers

    c. Popcorn

    d. Salted sunflower seeds

2. Pick a salty food:

    a. Pistachios

    b. Cheez-It crackers

    c. Tortilla chips

    d. Chex Mix

3. Pick a salty food:

    a. Peanut butter pretzels

    b. Soft pretzels

    c. Trail mix

    d. Cashew granola bar

4. Pick a salty food:

    a. Oyster crackers

    b. Salted caramel ice cream

    c. Chicken in a Biskit crackers

    d. Pretzel sticks

5. Pick a salty food:

a. Peanuts

b. Saltwater taffy

c. Potato chips

d. Mixed nuts

6. Pick a salty food:

a. Almonds

b. French fries

c. Ritz Crackers

d. Baked pita chips

• •

If you picked mostly As—you got Egg Peeler.

• You'd be peeling hard-boiled eggs to be packaged.

If you picked mostly Bs—you got Chewing Gum Taster.

• You'd be a taste tester for various gum flavors.

If you picked mostly Cs—you got Chicken Sexer.

• Your job is to figure out what sex chicks are.

If you picked mostly Ds—you got Dog Food Taster.

• You'd be a taste tester for various dog food flavors.

Based on the Cupcake Flavors You Choose, Which Disney Prince Should You Be With?

1. Choose a cupcake flavor:

- a. Raspberry
- b. Pistachio
- c. Funfetti

2. Choose a cupcake flavor:

- a. Chocolate
- b. Caramel pecan
- c. Cinnamon roll

3. Choose a cupcake flavor:

- a. Vanilla
- b. Carrot cake
- c. Boston cream

4. Choose a cupcake flavor:

- a. Lemon
- b. Blueberry
- c. Cookies and cream

5. Choose a cupcake flavor:

- a. Red velvet
- b. Key lime
- c. Strawberry

84

6. Choose a cupcake flavor:

a. Chocolate peanut butter

b. Banana

c. Orange Creamsicle

7. Choose a cupcake flavor:

a. Salted caramel

b. Chocolate raspberry

c. Rainbow sherbet

8. Choose a cupcake flavor:

a. Butterscotch

b. Toffee mocha

c. Maple bacon

9. Choose a cupcake flavor:

a. Black Forest

b. Chocolate hazelnut

c. Blueberry cheesecake

10. Choose a cupcake flavor:

a. Marble

b. Pumpkin

c. Snickerdoodle

• •

If you picked mostly As—you got John Smith from *Pocahontas*.

If you picked mostly Bs—you got Li Shang from *Mulan*.

If you picked mostly Cs—you got Prince Eric from *The Little Mermaid*.

Based on the Foods You Choose, Which State Do You Belong In?

1. Choose a breakfast food:

   a. Omelette

   b. Waffles

   c. Pancakes

   d. Yogurt parfait

   e. Cereal

   f. French toast sticks

2. Choose a bread:

   a. Corn bread

   b. Banana bread

   c. English muffin

   d. Garlic bread

   e. Dinner roll

   f. Biscuits

3. Choose a pasta:

   a. Baked ziti

   b. Spaghetti

   c. Fettuccine Alfredo

   d. Pesto gnocchi

   e. Mushroom Florentine

   f. Lasagna

4. Choose a cheesy food:

a. Mozzarella sticks

b. Chips and cheese

c. Cheeseburger

d. Macaroni and cheese

e. Grilled cheese sandwich

f. Cheesy breadsticks

5. Choose a sandwich:

a. Sloppy joe

b. Peanut butter and jelly

c. Breakfast

d. Ice cream

e. BLT

f. French dip

6. Choose a dessert:

a. Apple pie

b. Snickerdoodle cookie

c. Ice cream

d. Coconut pudding trifle

e. Butterscotch blondie

f. Chocolate lava cake

7. Choose a fruit:

a. Blueberries

b. Apple

c. Banana

d. Pineapple

e. Strawberries

f. Watermelon

Continued

8. Choose a vegetable:

   a. Corn

   b. Asparagus

   c. Carrot

   d. Broccoli

   e. Green peas

   f. Onion

9. Choose a junk food:

   a. Mini corn dog

   b. Chips

   c. Nachos

   d. Tater tots

   e. Pizza roll

   f. Chili cheese fries

• •

If you picked mostly As—you got Texas.

If you picked mostly Bs—you got Michigan.

If you picked mostly Cs—you got California.

If you picked mostly Ds—you got Hawaii.

If you picked mostly Es—you got Oregon.

If you picked mostly Fs—you got North Carolina.

Order Some Frozen Yogurt, and We'll Give You a Celebrity Boyfriend

1. Pick a first flavor:

  a. Cotton candy

  b. Blueberry

  c. Pumpkin

  d. Chocolate

  e. Vanilla

  f. Strawberry

2. Pick a second flavor:

  a. Cake batter

  b. Orange

  c. Mango

  d. Pineapple

  e. Peanut butter

  f. Salted caramel

3. Pick a third flavor:

  a. Cookies and cream

  b. Cinnamon

  c. Raspberry

  d. Cherry vanilla

  e. Red velvet

  f. I'm good with the flavors I have now

Continued

4. Pick a fruit topping:

a. Fruit on froyo? No thanks.

b. Bananas

c. Pomegranate seeds

d. Raspberries

e. Blueberries

f. Strawberries

5. How about some chocolate?

a. No chocolate for me

b. Reese's Peanut Butter Cups

c. Chocolate-covered pretzels

d. Crushed Heath Bar candy

e. Chocolate chips

f. No chocolate for me

6. Add another topping:

a. Mini marshmallows

b. Cheesecake bites

c. Peanuts

d. Cookie dough bites

e. Graham crackers

f. Butterscotch chips

7. Add another topping:

a. Froot Loops

b. Sour gummy worms

c. Rock candy

d. Frosted animal crackers

e. Nerds candy

f. None of these

8. Add another topping:

a. Sprinkles

b. Sour Patch Kids

c. Chocolate-covered raisins

d. Cookie pieces

e. Chocolate sauce

f. I don't want any more toppings

• •

If you picked mostly **As**—you got Justin Bieber.

If you picked mostly **Bs**—you got Michael B. Jordan.

If you picked mostly **Cs**—you got David Beckham.

If you picked mostly **Ds**—you got Theo James.

If you picked mostly **Es**—you got Zac Efron.

If you picked mostly **Fs**—you got Ryan Gosling.

Pick Your Favorite Sweets, and We'll Give You Something to Do This Summer

1. Pick a sweet:
a. Cinnamon roll

b. Vanilla cupcake

c. Frosted brownie

2. Pick a sweet:
a. Sour candy

b. Tiramisù

c. Chocolate meringue pie

3. Pick a sweet:
a. Butterscotch fudge

b. Mint chocolate chip ice cream

c. Cheesecake

4. Pick a sweet:
a. Oreo truffle

b. Ice cream sandwich

c. Pecan pie

5. Pick a sweet:
a. Funnel cake

b. S'mores parfait

c. Funfetti cupcake

6. Pick a sweet:

a. Chocolate lava cake

b. Sugar cookie

c. Strawberry ice cream

7. Pick a sweet:

a. Cinnamon sugar doughnut holes

b. Red velvet cake

c. Chocolate chip cookie

8. Pick a sweet:

a. Hot fudge sundae

b. Snickerdoodle cookie

c. Apple crumble

• •

If you picked mostly As—you should go to a fair.

If you picked mostly Bs—you should go on a road trip with friends.

If you picked mostly Cs—you should have a picnic.

Which Famous Family Do You Belong In?

1. Choose a breakfast food:
  a. Some form of eggs

  b. Fruit and yogurt

  c. Pancakes

2. Choose a food for lunch:
  a. Chicken and potatoes

  b. Salad

  c. Tacos

3. Choose something for dinner:
  a. Steak and fries

  b. Spaghetti

  c. Sloppy joe

4. Choose a pet:
  a. Cat

  b. Hamster

  c. Dog

5. Choose a movie:
  a. Any Marvel movie

  b. A romantic comedy

  c. Any Disney movie

6. Choose a board game:

a. The Game of Life

b. Monopoly

c. Candy Land

7. Choose somewhere to visit:

a. New York

b. France

c. Hawaii

8. Choose a sweet:

a. Cookies

b. Cheesecake

c. Brownie

9. Choose a TV show family to be a part of:

a. *The Simpsons*

b. *The Brady Bunch*

c. The Tanners from *Full House*

• •

If you picked mostly As—you got the Beckham family.

- It's a family of love, sports, and happiness.

If you picked mostly Bs—you got the Kardashian family.

- It's a family of love, drama, and fun times.

If you picked mostly Cs—you got the Obama family.

- It's a family of love, hard work, and time spent together.

Which Fictional Disney Land Should You Live In?

1. Choose a character from *The Lion King*:

  a. Pumbaa

  b. Mufasa

  c. Nala

  d. Simba

2. Choose a character from *A Bug's Life*:

  a. Heimlich

  b. Francis

  c. Princess Atta

  d. Flik

3. Choose a character from *The Incredibles*:

  a. Dash

  b. Mr. Incredible

  c. Elastigirl

  d. Jack-Jack

4. Choose a character from *Cars*:

  a. Flo

  b. Sally

  c. Lightning McQueen

  d. Mater

5. Choose a character from *Monsters, Inc.*:

a. Sully

b. Mike

c. Celia

d. Boo

6. Choose a character from *Snow White and the Seven Dwarfs*:

a. Bashful

b. Grumpy

c. Snow White

d. Dopey

7. Choose a character from *Finding Nemo*:

a. Nemo

b. Gill

c. Marlin

d. Dory

8. Choose a character from *Peter Pan*:

a. The Lost Boys

b. Mr. Smee

c. Tinker Bell

d. Peter Pan

9. Choose a character from *Aladdin*:

a. Rajah

b. Aladdin

c. Jasmine

d. Genie

Continued

10. Choose a character from *Beauty and the Beast*:

  a. Beast

  b. Lumière

  c. Belle

  d. Mrs. Potts

• •

If you picked mostly As—you got Zootopia from *Zootopia*.

If you picked mostly Bs—you got Radiator Springs from *Cars*.

If you picked mostly Cs—you got Te Fiti Island from *Moana*.

If you picked mostly Ds—you got Neverland from *Peter Pan*.

Based on Your Food Preferences, We'll Tell You Which Unusual Chip Flavor You Should Try

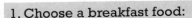

1. Choose a breakfast food:

a. Bacon

b. Bagel

c. Oatmeal

d. Smoothie

2. Choose a style of french fries:

a. Steak fries

b. Waffle fries

c. Curly fries

d. Standard fries

3. Choose a meat:

a. Ham

b. Turkey

c. Roast beef

d. No thanks

4. Choose a cookie flavor:

a. Frosted sugar

b. Peanut butter

c. Oatmeal raisin

d. Chocolate chip

Continued

5. Choose a bread:

a. Breadsticks

b. Pretzel

c. Banana bread

d. Baguette

6. Choose a healthy snack:

a. Apples and peanut butter

b. Bowl of fruit

c. Veggies and dip

d. Yogurt and granola

7. Choose an unhealthy snack:

a. Glazed doughnut

b. Cheese puffs

c. Sour candy

d. Ice cream

8. Choose a pizza topping:

a. Pepperoni

b. Extra cheese

c. Onions

d. Pineapples

9. Choose a classic food combination:

a. Bacon and eggs

b. Peanut butter and jelly sandwich

c. Chips and salsa

d. Spaghetti and meatballs

10. Choose a cuisine:

a. American food

b. Italian food

c. Chinese food

d. Mediterranean food

• •

If you picked mostly As—you got Pringles Pigs in a Blanket.

If you picked mostly Bs—you got Lay's Grilled Cheese & Ketchup.

If you picked mostly Cs—you got Lay's Kettle Cooked Wasabi Ginger.

If you picked mostly Ds—you got Lay's Cappuccino.

Which Latin American Food Matches Your Personality?

1. Pick a Mexican restaurant:

- a. Qdoba
- b. Chipotle Mexican Grill
- c. Taco Bell
- d. Del Taco

2. Pick a Latin American country:

- a. Chile
- b. Peru
- c. Guatemala
- d. Mexico

3. Pick a US state:

- a. Nevada
- b. Texas
- c. Wisconsin
- d. California

4. Pick a European country:

- a. Germany
- b. Greece
- c. Italy
- d. United Kingdom

5. Pick an outdoor activity:

- a. Mini golf
- b. Star gazing

c. Bike riding

d. Swimming

6. Pick an indoor activity:

a. Napping

b. Baking

c. Listening to music

d. Watching movies

7. Pick a season:

a. Winter

b. Fall

c. Spring

d. Summer

• •

If you picked mostly As—you got Tamale.

- You're peppy and don't fear much.

If you picked mostly Bs—you got Enchilada.

- You're one of a kind and very particular about things in your life. Organization and order are very important in your eyes.

If you picked mostly Cs—you got Quesadilla.

- You prefer not to stand out in a crowd; fitting in is perfectly fine for you.

If you picked mostly Ds—you got Taco.

- You love having fun and being with your loved ones.

Which Goldfish Crackers Match Your Personality?

1. Choose a movie:

    a. *The Wizard of Oz*

    b. *It*

    c. *13 Going on 30*

    d. *Jurassic Park*

    e. *The Lion King*

    f. *21 Jump Street*

2. Choose a discontinued snack:

    a. Keebler Fudge Magic Middles

    b. Planters Cheez Balls

    c. Keebler Ranch Munch 'Ems

    d. Doritos 3D

    e. Dunkaroos

    f. Butterfinger BB's

3. Choose a frozen food:

    a. Ore-Ida Golden Tater Tots

    b. TGI Friday's Mozzarella Sticks

    c. Kellogg's Eggo Waffles

    d. Stouffer's Macaroni & Cheese

    e. Kid Cuisine All Star Chicken Breast Nuggets

    f. Nestlé Toll House Chocolate Chip Cookie Sandwich

4. Choose a color:

a. Yellow

b. Purple

c. Green

d. Orange

e. Baby blue

f. Red

5. Choose a chip brand:

a. SunChips

b. Tostitos

c. Pringles

d. Cheetos

e. Doritos

f. Lay's

6. Choose an activity:

a. Napping

b. Watching TV

c. Playing sports

d. Swimming

e. Coloring

f. Dancing

7. Choose an item on the kids' menu:

a. Grilled chicken tenders

b. Hamburger

c. Grilled cheese

d. Macaroni and cheese

e. Corn dog

f. Chicken nuggets

Continued

8. Choose a Disney princess:

   a. Belle

   b. Jasmine

   c. Tiana

   d. Ariel

   e. Moana

   f. Rapunzel

9. Choose a type of fish:

   a. Swordfish

   b. Puffer fish

   c. Blue tang

   d. Goldfish

   e. Clownfish

   f. Rainbow trout

● ●

If you picked mostly As—you got Parmesan Goldfish Crackers.

- You're mature and passionate.

If you picked mostly Bs—you got Pretzel Goldfish Crackers.

- You're strong-willed and entertaining.

If you picked mostly Cs—you got French Toast Goldfish Grahams.

- You're outgoing and you very deeply value your relationships with your loved ones.

If you picked mostly Ds—you got Cheddar Goldfish Crackers.

- You're a kindhearted person.

If you picked mostly Es—you got Baby Cheddar Goldfish Crackers.

- You're immature at times, but people know they can always turn to you for a good time.

If you picked mostly Fs—you got Colors Goldfish Crackers.

- You're lively and you give off confidence.

Which Halloween Song Matches Your Personality?

1. Pick a holiday:

    a. Valentine's Day

    b. Christmas

    c. Thanksgiving

2. Pick a Halloween costume to wear:

    a. Gorilla suit

    b. Sheet ghost

    c. Crayon

3. Pick a pet costume:

    a. Spider

    b. Prisoner

    c. Hot dog

4. Pick a party theme:

    a. '80s

    b. Murder mystery

    c. Costume

5. Pick a fall food:

    a. Mashed sweet potatoes

    b. Caramel apples

    c. Apple cider doughnuts

6. Pick a fall activity:

a. Going to a football game

b. Picking apples

c. Going to a corn maze

7. Pick a season:

a. Summer

b. Winter

c. Fall

8. Pick a movie genre:

a. Family-friendly

b. Sci-fi

c. Horror

9. Pick a band:

a. Led Zeppelin

b. 5 Seconds of Summer

c. The Beatles

• •

If you picked mostly As—you got "Monster Mash" by Bobby "Boris" Pickett.

If you picked mostly Bs—you got "Ghostbusters" by Ray Parker Jr.

If you picked mostly Cs—you got "This Is Halloween" by the cast of *The Nightmare Before Christmas*.

Which Type of Penguin Matches Your Personality?

1. Choose a job:

  a. Actor/actress

  b. Dancer

  c. Photographer

2. Choose a color:

  a. Purple

  b. Blue

  c. Black

3. Choose a celebrity:

  a. Drake

  b. Kendall Jenner

  c. Demi Lovato

4. Choose a winter activity:

  a. Snowboarding

  b. Ice skating

  c. Sledding

5. Which sport do you hate the most?:

  a. Tennis

  b. Soccer

  c. Football

6. Choose an ice cream sundae:

   a. Chocolate

   b. Strawberry

   c. Caramel

7. Choose a Justin Bieber song:

   a. "Never Say Never"

   b. "Love Yourself"

   c. "I'm the One"

• •

If you picked mostly As—you got Emperor Penguin.

   • You're a leader.

If you picked mostly Bs—you got Chinstrap Penguin.

   • You're a follower.

If you picked mostly Cs—you got Crested Penguin.

   • You don't like being told what to do.

Which Type of Hot Dog Matches Your Personality?

1. Which of these is your favorite social media platform?

    a. Instagram

    b. Snapchat

    c. Facebook

    d. YouTube

2. Which of these sandwiches sounds tastiest?

    a. Hamburger

    b. BLT

    c. Sloppy joe

    d. Grilled cheese

3. Which of these is your favorite singer?

    a. Taylor Swift

    b. Bruno Mars

    c. Rihanna

    d. Post Malone

4. How would your friends describe you?

    a. Casual

    b. Sarcastic

    c. Bold

    d. Crazy

5. Which of these is your favorite condiment?

    a. Ketchup

    b. Mustard

c. Relish

d. Barbecue sauce

6. Which is your favorite kind of bread?

a. White

b. Whole wheat

c. Rye

d. Whole grain

7. Which of these would you put on your bucket list?

a. Meet your favorite celebrity

b. Travel out of the country

c. Go skydiving

d. Win a hot dog–eating contest

8. Which of these is your favorite scents?

a. Vanilla

b. Lavender

c. Bacon

d. Chocolate

9. Which of these careers do you think you'd be best at?

a. Teacher

b. Travel writer

c. Movie producer

d. Cake decorator

10. Which of these is your favorite dog breed?

a. Golden retriever

b. Dachshund

c. Pug

d. Pomeranian   *Continued*

• •

If you picked mostly As—you got Regular Hot Dog.

- You're typical and focus on the essentials in life.

If you picked mostly Bs—you got Foot-Long Hot Dog.

- You always love to go the extra mile in life. You don't enjoy just being average.

If you picked mostly Cs—you got Chili Dog.

- You hate simplicity and want to go through life in a fun and unique way.

If you picked mostly Ds—you got Corn Dog.

- You're a kid at heart and love attention from others.

Which Gummy Bear Flavor Matches Your Personality?

1. Pick a sweet treat:

- a. Soft-serve ice cream
- b. Mini cupcakes
- c. Cotton candy
- d. Frosted sugar cookies
- e. Brownies

2. Pick a letter of the alphabet:

- a. X
- b. U
- c. I
- d. S
- e. J

3. Pick a cartoon character:

- a. Tweety Bird
- b. Ferb Fletcher
- c. Bart Simpson
- d. Scooby-Doo
- e. SpongeBob SquarePants

4. Pick a career:

- a. Interior designer
- b. Nurse
- c. Writer
- d. Actor
- e. Teacher

115

Continued

5. Pick some candy:

a. Tropical Sour Patch Kids

b. Skittles

c. Lemonheads

d. Jelly beans

e. Jolly Ranchers

6. Pick a school subject:

a. Art

b. Science

c. History

d. English

e. Math

7. Pick a muffin flavor:

a. Blueberry

b. Banana

c. Poppy seed

d. Chocolate chip

e. Apple cinnamon

8. Pick a fast-food restaurant:

a. In-N-Out Burger

b. Qdoba

c. Sonic

d. McDonald's

e. Wendy's

9. Pick a bear:

a. Sloth bear

b. Panda bear

c. Polar bear

d. Gummy bear

e. Brown bear

• •

If you picked mostly As—you got Pineapple Gummy Bear.

> • You're unique, and you don't let anyone walk over you or your friends.

If you picked mostly Bs—you got Orange Gummy Bear.

> • You're a friendly face that people always love to see.

If you picked mostly Cs—you got Lemon Gummy Bear.

> • You're not one to fall into line and go with the crowd; you like being different.

If you picked mostly Ds—you got Cherry Gummy Bear.

> • You're a simple soul, and people love that about you.

If you picked mostly Es—you got Green Apple Gummy Bear.

> • You're passionate about many things, and you always let people know how much you care for them.

Which Black-and-White Animal Matches Your Personality?

1. Pick some macaroni and cheese:

a. Garlic Parmesan

b. Bacon

c. Shell

d. Regular

2. Pick a black-and-white item:

a. Newspaper

b. Soccer ball

c. Checkered flag

d. Oreo

3. Pick a color:

a. Pink

b. Red

c. Orange

d. Green

4. Pick a school elective:

a. Graphic design

b. Home economics

c. Aerobics

d. Photography

5. Pick something that gets on your nerves:

a. Cracking your phone screen

b. Cold fries

c. Going to the bathroom and there's no toilet paper

d. No Wi-Fi

6. Pick a beverage never to drink again:

a. Pop

b. Tea

c. Coffee

d. Beer

7. Pick an aquatic animal:

a. Dolphin

b. Manatee

c. Whale

d. Octopus

• •

If you picked mostly As—you got Zebra.

- You're all about your friends and family and showing them how much you care.

If you picked mostly Bs—you got Cow.

- You tend to be lazy, but you have a lot of passion.

If you picked mostly Cs—you got Killer Whale.

- You're feisty and fight for what you believe and want.

If you picked mostly Ds—you got Giant Panda.

- You're best friends with the couch and your room. Relaxation time and alone time are crucial for you.

Which Constellation Matches Your Personality?

1. Pick a drink:
a. Lemonade

b. Coffee

c. Water

2. Pick a neon color:
a. Neon green

b. Neon orange

c. Neon pink

3. Pick an activity:
a. Reading

b. Drawing

c. Dancing

4. Pick a shape:
a. Square

b. Circle

c. Triangle

5. Pick a sport:
a. Soccer

b. Gymnastics

c. Basketball

6. Pick a game:
a. The Game of Life

b. Uno

c. Mario Kart

7. Pick a cartoon character:

a. Winnie the Pooh

b. Donald Duck

c. Scooby-Doo

8. Pick a food:

a. Pizza

b. Tacos

c. Burgers

9. Pick a word to describe yourself:

a. Basic

b. Unique

c. Fun

• •

If you picked mostly As—you got Lyra.

- This northern constellation represents the lyre, an ancient musical instrument that resembles a small harp.

If you picked mostly Bs—you got Draco.

- You can find this constellation in the far northern sky. Its name is Latin for "dragon."

If you picked mostly Cs—you got Ursa Major.

- This constellation is found in the northern sky. Its name means "the great bear" or "the larger bear" in Latin, and it is more commonly known as "The Big Dipper."

Which Cotton Candy Flavor Matches Your Personality?

1. Pick a TV show:

   a. *Modern Family*

   b. *New Girl*

   c. *Gossip Girl*

2. Pick a fair food:

   a. Popcorn

   b. French fries

   c. Funnel cake

3. Pick a winter activity:

   a. Sledding

   b. Ice skating

   c. Snowmobiling

4. Pick a summer activity:

   a. Camping

   b. Bike riding

   c. Tubing

5. Pick a mythical creature:

   a. Mermaid

   b. Fairy

   c. Unicorn

6. Pick a *Friends* character:

a. Rachel

b. Phoebe

c. Joey

7. Pick a round food:

a. Waffle

b. Doughnut

c. Pizza

8. Pick a cartoon character:

a. Piglet

b. Timmy Turner

c. Goofy

• •

If you picked mostly As—you got Blue Raspberry.

- You're laid back but can perk up in the right situation. You're hardworking, you love hanging out at home, and you love spending time with your family.

If you picked mostly Bs—you got Strawberry.

- You have a quirky personality, and your friends and family love you for it. You're a social butterfly, and people always gravitate toward you.

If you picked mostly Cs—you got Grape.

- You're the life of the party! Your friends can always count on you for a good time, but they also know you're the perfect friend to turn to when they're going through a rough time.

Which Dr. Seuss Quote Matches Your Personality?

1. Choose a Dr. Seuss book:

a. *Green Eggs and Ham*

b. *One Fish, Two Fish, Red Fish, Blue Fish*

c. *Oh, the Places You'll Go!*

d. *The Cat in the Hat*

2. Choose an animal:

a. Hamster

b. Parrot

c. Cheetah

d. Zebra

3. Choose an ice cream flavor:

a. Vanilla

b. Cotton candy

c. Chocolate fudge

d. Cookies and cream

4. Choose a school subject:

a. Science

b. Art

c. Math

d. English

5. Choose a salad:

a. Caesar salad

b. Taco salad

c. Pasta salad

d. Potato salad

6. Choose a color:

a. Blue

b. Green

c. Red

d. Yellow

7. Choose a cookie:

a. Chocolate chip

b. Snickerdoodle

c. Peanut butter

d. Sugar

8. Choose a flower:

a. Daisy

b. Sunflower

c. Tulip

d. Rose

9. Choose a Dr. Seuss character:

a. Thing One and Thing Two from *The Cat in the Hat*

b. Horton from *Horton Hears a Who!*

c. The Lorax from *The Lorax*

d. The Grinch from *How the Grinch Stole Christmas!*

Continued

• •

If you picked mostly As—you got "A person's a person, no matter how small."

If you picked mostly Bs—you got "Why fit in when you were born to stand out?"

If you picked mostly Cs—you got "You're off to great places! Today is your day! Your mountain is waiting, so . . . get on your way!"

If you picked mostly Ds—you got "Today you are You, that is truer than true. There is no one alive that is Youer than You."

Which Fruit Matches Your Personality?

1. Choose your favorite social media platform:

  a. Twitter

  b. Instagram

  c. Snapchat

  d. YouTube

  e. Facebook

  f. Pinterest

2. Choose a breakfast food:

  a. Scrambled eggs on toast

  b. Muffin

  c. Bagel

  d. Waffles

  e. Cereal

  f. Cinnamon French toast sticks

3. Choose a school subject:

  a. Art

  b. English

  c. Science

  d. Gym

  e. History

  f. Math

Continued

4. Choose a salty food:

a. Almonds

b. Soft pretzel

c. Cashews

d. Potato chips

e. French fries

f. Popcorn

5. Choose a milkshake flavor:

a. Orange cream

b. Vanilla

c. Caramel

d. Peanut butter cup

e. Cookies and cream

f. Chocolate

6. Choose a fruity dessert:

a. Lemon cake

b. Strawberry shortcake

c. Key lime pie

d. Blueberry doughnuts

e. Apple crisp

f. Peach cobbler

7. Choose a vegetable:

a. Celery

b. Carrots

c. Broccoli

d. Peas

e. Corn

f. Potatoes

8. Choose a fruity candy:

a. Sour Patch Kids

b. Jelly beans

c. Laffy Taffy

d. Mike and Ike

e. Starbursts

f. Skittles

• •

If you picked mostly As—you got Lemon.

• In one word: you're spunky.

If you picked mostly Bs—you got Strawberry.

• In one word: you're thoughtful.

If you picked mostly Cs—you got Kiwi.

• In one word: you're unique.

If you picked mostly Ds—you got Blueberry.

• In one word: you're admirable.

If you picked mostly Es—you got Apple.

• In one word: you're friendly.

If you picked mostly Fs—you got Peach.

• In one word: you're compassionate.

Based on How You Rate These Ice Cream Flavors, We'll Match You with a Celebrity Bestie

1. How do you feel about vanilla ice cream?

a. Yuck

b. Yum

c. Indifferent

2. How do you feel about chocolate ice cream?

a. Yuck

b. Yum

c. Indifferent

3. How do you feel about mint chocolate chip ice cream?

a. Yuck

b. Yum

c. Indifferent

4. How do you feel about butter pecan ice cream?

a. Yuck

b. Yum

c. Indifferent

5. How do you feel about Neapolitan ice cream?

a. Yuck

b. Yum

c. Indifferent

6. How do you feel about strawberry ice cream?

  a. Yuck

  b. Yum

  c. Indifferent

7. How do you feel about chocolate chip cookie dough ice cream?

  a. Yuck

  b. Yum

  c. Indifferent

8. How do you feel about black cherry ice cream?

  a. Yuck

  b. Yum

  c. Indifferent

9. How do you feel about cookies and cream ice cream?

  a. Yuck

  b. Yum

  c. Indifferent

10. How do you feel about cotton candy ice cream?

  a. Yuck

  b. Yum

  c. Indifferent

• •

If you picked mostly **As**—you got **Cole Sprouse.**

If you picked mostly **Bs**—you got **Rebel Wilson.**

If you picked mostly **Cs**—you got **Zooey Deschanel.**

Based on How You Answer These Questions, We'll Match You with a Cartoon BFF

1. Choose a Cartoon Network show:

a. *Ed, Edd n Eddy*

b. *Codename: Kids Next Door*

c. *Courage the Cowardly Dog*

2. Choose some candy:

a. Sour Patch Kids

b. Werther's Original Hard Caramels

c. Reese's Pieces

3. Choose an animal:

a. Hyena

b. Horse

c. Sloth

4. Choose a food:

a. Pizza

b. Sushi

c. Chicken nuggets

5. Choose a place to spend the weekend:

a. At an amusement park

b. At the beach

c. At a friend's house

6. Choose a scent:

   a. Barbecue

   b. Lavender

   c. Baked cookies

7. Choose a cartoon kid:

   a. Charlie Brown from *Peanuts*

   b. Dora from *Dora the Explorer*

   c. Chuckie Finster from *Rugrats*

• •

If you picked mostly As—you got Bart Simpson from *The Simpsons*.

If you picked mostly Bs—you got Blossom from *The Powerpuff Girls*.

If you picked mostly Cs—you got Shaggy Rogers from *Scooby-Doo, Where Are You!*

Which Fictional Cat Matches Your Personality?

1. Pick a cartoon BFF:

   a. Sheriff Woody Pride from *Toy Story*

   b. Patrick Star from *SpongeBob SquarePants*

   c. Timmy Turner from *The Fairly OddParents*

   d. Mickey Mouse from *Mickey Mouse Clubhouse*

2. Pick a school subject:

   a. Math

   b. English

   c. Science

   d. History

3. Pick a social media platform:

   a. YouTube

   b. Facebook

   c. Tumblr

   d. Pinterest

4. Pick a game:

   a. Twister

   b. Apples to Apples

   c. Uno

   d. Bingo

5. Pick a coffee:

a. Iced

b. Cappuccino

c. Black

d. None for me

6. Pick a candy:

a. Candy corn

b. Snickers bar

c. M&M's

d. SweeTarts

7. Pick a funny movie:

a. *Tag*

b. *Deadpool*

c. *Step Brothers*

d. *Napoleon Dynamite*

• •

If you picked mostly As—you got Puss in Boots from *Shrek 2*.

If you picked mostly Bs—you got Garfield from *Garfield and Friends*.

If you picked mostly Cs—you got the Cheshire Cat from *Alice in Wonderland*.

If you picked mostly Ds—you got Figaro from *Pinocchio*.

Which Type of Corgi Matches Your Personality?

1. Pick a food:

   a. Peanut butter

   b. Bananas

   c. Cheese

2. Pick a dog breed:

   a. Golden retriever

   b. Labrador retriever

   c. Border collie

3. What time do you normally wake up?

   a. Before 7 a.m.

   b. Between 8 and 9 a.m.

   c. 10 a.m. or later

4. Pick an animal:

   a. Pug

   b. Donkey

   c. Squirrel

5. Pick a game:

   a. Tag

   b. Hide-and-seek

   c. Capture the flag

6. Pick a word to describe yourself:

a. Basic

b. Bold

c. Unique

7. Pick a famous royal:

a. Princess Diana

b. Queen Elizabeth

c. Prince William

8. Pick a color:

a. Black

b. Blue

c. Red

• •

If you picked mostly As—you got Pembroke Welsh Corgi.

- You're not simple-minded, but you do tend to go with the crowd and follow trends.

If you picked mostly Bs—you got Blue Merle Corgi.

- You're energetic and love trying new things.

If you picked mostly Cs—you got Red Merle Corgi.

- You're quick to judge not just others but also yourself.

Which *Scooby-Doo* Character Matches Your Personality?

1. Pick a talk-show host:

    a. James Corden

    b. Dr. Phil

    c. Jimmy Kimmel

    d. Ellen DeGeneres

    e. Jimmy Fallon

2. Pick an activity:

    a. Going out to eat

    b. Reading

    c. Playing a sport

    d. Hanging with friends

    e. Having a spa day

3. Pick a condiment:

    a. Ranch dressing

    b. Mustard

    c. Mayonnaise

    d. Barbecue sauce

    e. Ketchup

4. Pick a drink:

    a. Milk

    b. Water

    c. Pop

    d. Lemonade

    e. Iced coffee

5. Pick a dog breed:

    a. Golden retriever

    b. Dachshund

    c. Siberian husky

    d. Australian shepherd

    e. Shih Tzu

6. Pick an appetizer:

    a. Maple and brown sugar bacon–wrapped hot dogs

    b. Chips and salsa

    c. Barbecue meatballs

    d. Mozzarella sticks

    e. Veggies and dip

7. Pick a random food:

    a. French fries

    b. Caramel popcorn

    c. Chocolate melting cake

    d. Blueberry pancakes

    e. Raspberry cupcakes

• •

If you picked mostly **As**—you got Scooby-Doo.

If you picked mostly **Bs**—you got Velma Dinkley.

If you picked mostly **Cs**—you got Fred Jones.

If you picked mostly **Ds**—you got Shaggy Rogers.

If you picked mostly **Es**—you got Daphne Blake.

Which Droid from *Star Wars* Matches Your Personality?

1. Pick a *Star Wars* character:

  a. Yoda

  b. Rey

  c. Luke Skywalker

  d. Princess Leia

  e. Han Solo

2. Pick a shape:

  a. Triangle

  b. Circle

  c. Oval

  d. Rectangle

  e. Square

3. Pick a gemstone:

  a. Amber

  b. Pearl

  c. Sapphire

  d. Ruby

  e. Emerald

4. Pick a mode of transportation:

  a. Car

  b. Bike

  c. Plane

d. Train

e. Boat

5. Pick an electronic item:

a. Camera

b. iPhone

c. Laptop

d. Flat-screen TV

e. Gaming system

6. Pick a number:

a. 3

b. 8

c. 2

d. 37

e. 100

7. Pick a robot:

a. The Iron Giant from *The Iron Giant*

b. WALL-E from *WALL-E*

c. Goddard from *Jimmy Neutron: Boy Genius*

d. Bender from *Futurama*

e. Astro Boy from *Astro Boy*

• •

If you picked mostly As—you got C-3PO.

If you picked mostly Bs—you got BB-8.

If you picked mostly Cs—you got R2-D2.

If you picked mostly Ds—you got L3-37.

If you picked mostly Es—you got Battle Droid.

Which Jim Carrey Character Matches Your Personality?

1. Choose a holiday:

   a. Halloween

   b. Christmas

   c. Valentine's Day

   d. Thanksgiving

2. Choose a meal:

   a. Breakfast

   b. Lunch

   c. Dinner

   d. Dessert

3. Choose a job:

   a. Unemployed

   b. Veterinarian

   c. Lawyer

   d. Business owner

4. Choose a travel destination:

   a. Alaska

   b. Sydney

   c. New York City

   d. London

5. Choose an animal:

a. Dog

b. Dolphin

c. Monkey

d. Seal

6. Choose a drink:

a. Milk

b. Beer

c. Pop

d. Water

7. Choose an actor:

a. Will Ferrell

b. Adam Sandler

c. Chris Rock

d. Jonah Hill

• •

If you picked mostly As—you got the Grinch from *How the Grinch Stole Christmas*.

If you picked mostly Bs—you got Ace Ventura from *Ace Ventura: Pet Detective*.

If you picked mostly Cs—you got Fletcher Reede from *Liar Liar*.

If you picked mostly Ds—you got Mr. Popper from *Mr. Popper's Penguins*.

Which Cartoon Family Do You Belong In?

1. Which of these buffets would you like to go to?

a. Pizza buffet

b. Pasta buffet

c. Breakfast buffet

2. Choose an odd talent you wish you had:

a. The ability to drink with your feet

b. The ability to talk backward

c. The ability to do eyebrow dancing

3. Choose a name:

a. Troy

b. Stacy

c. Chloe

4. Choose a board game:

a. Mouse Trap

b. Sorry!

c. Candy Land

5. Choose a candy never to eat again:

a. Gumdrops

b. Gummy bears

c. Jelly beans

6. Choose some bread:

a. Cheesy breadsticks

b. Garlic knots

c. Cinnamon toast

7. Choose a cartoon animal:

a. Brian from *Family Guy*

b. Swiper from *Dora the Explorer*

c. Max from *Max & Ruby*

8. Choose a cake:

a. Funfetti cake

b. Cheesecake

c. Chocolate cake

• •

If you picked mostly As—you got the Simpsons from *The Simpsons*.

If you picked mostly Bs—you got the Flynns and Fletchers from *Phineas and Ferb*.

If you picked mostly Cs—you got the Turners from *The Fairly OddParents*.

Which of the Great Lakes Matches Your Personality?

1. Pick a water activity:

a. Kayaking

b. Boating

c. Tubing

d. Surfing

e. Swimming

2. Pick a water:

a. Lemon water

b. Wild berry–flavored water

c. Regular water

d. Vitamin water

e. Sparkling water

3. Pick someone to spend the day with:

a. Your cousin

b. Your pet

c. Your best friend

d. Your sibling

e. Your mom

4. Pick a celebrity to spend the day with:

a. Chris Pratt

b. Zendaya

c. Ellen DeGeneres

d. Zac Efron

e. Blake Lively

5. Pick something you wish you had:

a. More money

b. A yacht

c. A cottage

d. A jet ski

e. A jet

6. Pick a snack:

a. Almonds

b. Cheez-It crackers

c. Potato chips

d. Mini sandwiches

e. Fruit kabobs

7. Pick an ocean:

a. Pacific Ocean

b. Southern Ocean

c. Atlantic Ocean

d. Indian Ocean

e. Arctic Ocean

• •

If you picked mostly As—you got Lake Huron.

• You're the second-largest Great Lake. You feel that money is a key to happiness.

If you picked mostly Bs—you got Lake Ontario.

• You're the smallest of the Great Lakes. You cherish your alone time.   *Continued*

If you picked mostly Cs—you got Lake Michigan.

- You're in the middle when it comes to the sizes of the Great Lakes. You take time off and use it to your best advantage.

If you picked mostly Ds—you got Lake Erie.

- You're the second-smallest of the Great Lakes. You're a big family person.

If you picked mostly Es—you got Lake Superior.

- You're the biggest of the Great Lakes. You like to go big or go home.

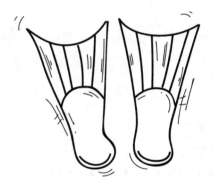

Which *Looney Tunes* Character Matches Your Personality?

1. Pick something for breakfast:

a. Scrambled eggs

b. Waffles

c. Blueberry pancakes

d. Breakfast sandwich

e. Doughnut

2. Pick something for lunch:

a. Salad

b. Tacos

c. Macaroni and cheese

d. Pizza

e. Chicken nuggets

3. Pick something for dinner:

a. Spaghetti

b. Paella

c. Steak

d. Chili

e. Meat loaf

Continued

4. Pick a color:

a. Yellow

b. Orange

c. Gray

d. Red

e. Pink

5. Pick an animal:

a. Otter

b. Flamingo

c. Kangaroo

d. Bear

e. Sloth

6. Pick a word:

a. Yellow

b. Unusual

c. Bouncy

d. Crazy

e. Chunky

7. Pick a TV show:

a. *Rugrats*

b. *Futurama*

c. *Phineas and Ferb*

d. *Bob's Burgers*

e. *Scooby-Doo, Where Are You!*

8. Pick a cookie:

a. Dark chocolate

b. Peanut butter

c. Chocolate chip

d. Sugar

e. Snickerdoodle

9. Pick a movie genre:

a. Romance

b. Comedy

c. Action

d. Horror

e. Sci-fi

• •

If you picked mostly As—you got Tweety Bird.

If you picked mostly Bs—you got Daffy Duck.

If you picked mostly Cs—you got Bugs Bunny.

If you picked mostly Ds—you got the Tasmanian Devil.

If you picked mostly Es—you got Porky Pig.

Which Flavor of Doritos Matches Your Personality?

1. Pick a dip:

a. French onion dip

b. Salsa

c. Queso

2. Pick another brand of chips:

a. Pringles

b. Cheetos

c. Lay's

3. Pick some potatoes:

a. French fries

b. Mashed sweet potatoes

c. Cheesy potatoes

4. Pick a color:

a. Blue

b. Orange

c. Red

5. Pick a movie genre:

a. Romantic comedy

b. Action

c. Comedy

6. Pick a pet:

   a. Cat

   b. Dog

   c. Both

7. Pick a made-up ice cream flavor:

   a. Chicken tenders

   b. Burrito

   c. Pizza

● ●

If you picked mostly As—you got Cool Ranch Doritos.

   • You're passionate and interesting.

If you picked mostly Bs—you got Spicy Nacho Doritos.

   • You're determined and vocal.

If you picked mostly Cs—you got Nacho Cheese Doritos.

   • You're cheesy and amusing.

Which Children's Book Matches Your Personality?

1. Which word describes you the best?

a. Hungry

b. Loving

c. Clueless

d. Unique

2. What's something you'd put on your bucket list?

a. Winning a pie-eating contest

b. Going on a pilgrimage

c. Peeing in every ocean

d. Being hypnotized

3. Which of these was your least favorite school subject?

a. English

b. Gym

c. Math

d. Science

4. Which of these is your favorite color?

a. Lime green

b. Dark green

c. Baby blue

d. Dark blue

5. Which of these is your favorite genre of books?

  a. Fiction

  b. Nonfiction

  c. Graphic novel

  d. Mystery

6. Choose a Dr. Seuss book:

  a. *Green Eggs and Ham*

  b. *Oh, the Places You'll Go!*

  c. *The Foot Book*

  d. *Horton Hears a Who!*

• •

If you picked mostly As—you got *The Very Hungry Caterpillar* by Eric Carle.

If you picked mostly Bs—you got *The Giving Tree* by Shel Silverstein.

If you picked mostly Cs—you got *Don't Let the Pigeon Drive the Bus!* by Mo Willems.

If you picked mostly Ds—you got *The Rainbow Fish* by Marcus Pfister.

Which Famous Roommates Would You Fit In Best With?

1. Choose a place to live:

   a. Los Angeles

   b. New York City

   c. Chicago

   d. Nashville

2. Choose some takeout to bring home to your roomies:

   a. Chinese food

   b. Pizza

   c. Burgers and fries

   d. Mexican food

3. Which word describes you best?

   a. Messy

   b. Friendly

   c. Childish

   d. Charming

4. Choose a cartoon character to be your best friend:

   a. Philip J. Fry from *Futurama*

   b. Snow White from *Snow White and the Seven Dwarfs*

   c. Boots from *Dora the Explorer*

   d. Daphne Blake from *Scooby-Doo, Where Are You!*

5. Choose a color to paint your room:

   a. Blue

   b. Light purple

c. Gray

d. Yellow

6. Where in your home is your favorite place to be?

a. On the living-room couch

b. In the kitchen

c. Outside

d. In your room

7. Choose something you and your roomies love to do:

a. Roast each other

b. Go out together

c. Talk about one another's problems

d. Watch TV shows

8. Choose something you hate:

a. Being alone

b. Drama

c. Selfish people

d. Messy people

● ●

If you picked mostly As—you got Jess, Nick, Winston, and Schmidt from *New Girl*.

If you picked mostly Bs—you got Monica and Rachel from *Friends*.

If you picked mostly Cs—you got Bert and Ernie from *Sesame Street*.

If you picked mostly Ds—you got Jack Tripper, Janet Wood, and Chrissy Snow from *Three's Company*.

Which Flavor of Baked Beans Matches Your Personality?

1. Which is your weakness?

a. Puppies

b. Babies

c. Kittens

2. Are you close to your family?

a. Yes

b. Mostly

c. Not really

3. What is your favorite color combination?

a. Red and blue

b. Pink and green

c. Purple and orange

4. Do you prefer routine or spontaneity?

a. Spontaneity

b. Routine

c. It depends on the day

5. Choose a song:

a. "Sweet Home Alabama" by Lynyrd Skynyrd

b. "Here Comes the Sun" by the Beatles

c. "Rocket Man" by Elton John

6. Which two words best describe you?

a. Clever and hot

b. Sweet and intelligent

c. Fun and caring

7. Choose a jelly bean flavor:

a. Cherry

b. Lemon

c. Grape

• •

If you picked mostly As—you got Barbecue Baked Beans.

• You're a basic kind of bean. You're all about good
  times and eating good foods.

**If you picked mostly Bs—you got Honey Sweet Baked
Beans.**

• You're a sweet kind of bean. You're caring and loving.

**If you picked mostly Cs—you got Brown Sugar Hickory
Baked Beans.**

• You're a savory kind of bean. You have determination
  and drive.

Which Fried Food Matches Your Personality?

1. Choose a social media platform:

a. Facebook

b. Twitter

c. Snapchat

d. Instagram

2. Choose a sport:

a. Soccer

b. Football

c. Gymnastics

d. Baseball

3. Choose the word you hate the most:

a. Curd

b. Yolk

c. Moist

d. Phlegm

4. Choose a party theme:

a. Hawaiian

b. Sports

c. Carnival

d. Costume

5. Choose a food:

a. Roast chicken

b. Mashed potatoes

c. Dinner rolls

d. Corn on the cob

6. Choose a holiday figure:

a. Rudolph the Red-Nosed Reindeer

b. Santa Claus

c. Easter Bunny

d. St. Patrick's Day leprechaun

7. Choose a college major:

a. Marine biology

b. Sports marketing

c. Communications

d. Physical therapy

• •

If you picked mostly As—you got Fish Sticks.

- You're all about others.

If you picked mostly Bs—you got Onion Rings.

- You're all about profiting and doing the best for yourself.

If you picked mostly Cs—you got Churros.

- You're all about socializing.

If you picked mostly Ds—you got Fried Pickles.

- You're all about well-being.

Which Famous Group Would You Fit In Best With?

1. Choose a sitcom:

a. *Modern Family*

b. *The Simpsons*

c. *M*A*S*H*

d. *The Fresh Prince of Bel-Air*

2. Choose a famous duo:

a. The Blues Brothers

b. Tom and Jerry

c. Batman and Robin

d. Sonny and Cher

3. Choose a famous trio:

a. The Ghostbusters

b. The Powerpuff Girls

c. Luke Skywalker, Princess Leia, and Han Solo

d. Destiny's Child

4. Choose a something to be good at:

a. Playing an instrument

b. Investigating

c. Karate

d. Dancing

5. Choose a US destination to visit:

a. Las Vegas

b. Grand Canyon

c. New York City

d. New Orleans

6. Choose a drink:

a. Blue raspberry slushie

b. Sprite

c. Water

d. Piña colada

7. Choose a band:

a. Queen

b. One Direction

c. The Beatles

d. Maroon 5

• •

If you picked mostly As—you got Blue Man Group.

If you picked mostly Bs—you got Scooby-Doo! Mystery Incorporated.

If you picked mostly Cs—you got the Fantastic Four from *Fantastic Four*.

If you picked mostly Ds—you got the Barden Bellas from *Pitch Perfect*.

Which Type of Pizza Matches Your Personality?

1. Pick a pizza topping:
a. Pineapple

b. Sausage

c. Tomato

d. Pepperoni

2. Pick a sport:
a. Baseball

b. Soccer

c. Tennis

d. Football

3. Pick a food:
a. Pop-Tarts

b. Loaf of bread

c. Quiche

d. Pie

4. Pick a cheese:
a. Mozzarella

b. Parmesan

c. Smoked Gouda

d. Cheddar Jack

5. Pick a circular food:
a. Pancake

b. Potato smile

c. Cookie

d. Doughnut

6. Pick a describing word:

a. Sweet

b. Salty

c. Savory

d. Creamy

7. Pick a shape:

a. Square

b. Circle

c. Triangle

d. Rectangle

● ●

If you picked mostly As—you got Thin-Crust Pizza.

- You're lighthearted and admire those who always do what they love, no matter what.

If you picked mostly Bs—you got Sicilian Pizza.

- You're determined and don't really care if people don't like you because you like yourself.

If you picked mostly Cs—you got Neapolitan Pizza.

- You're well mannered and love spending time with your loved ones.

If you picked mostly Ds—you got Deep-Dish Pizza.

- You have many layers, and you don't reveal them to anyone until you fully trust that person.

4

This or That?

Are You a Cheeseburger or a Hamburger?

1. Pick a color combination:
- a. Blue and green
- b. Red and orange

2. Choose an activity:
- a. Watching a movie
- b. Bowling

3. Pick some chips:
- a. Lay's Classic
- b. Doritos Nacho Cheese

4. Choose a Disney movie:
- a. *The Little Mermaid*
- b. *Finding Nemo*

5. Choose a beverage:
- a. Lemonade
- b. Chocolate milkshake

6. Choose a sport:
- a. Baseball
- b. Football

7. Choose a cartoon TV show:
- a. *SpongeBob SquarePants*
- b. *Family Guy*

Continued

8. Choose a cinnamon-based food:

a. Cinnamon rolls

b. Cinnamon French toast sticks

9. Choose an animal:

a. Dog

b. Dolphin

10. Choose a food that starts with P:

a. Pasta

b. Pancakes

11. Choose a job:

a. Teacher

b. Actor

12. Choose a vacation destination:

a. Paris

b. Los Angeles

13. Do you believe in ghosts?

a. No

b. Yes

14. How do you pronounce "caramel"?

a. "Care-a-mel"

b. "Car-mull"

15. Choose a side to eat with a hamburger or cheeseburger:

a. Corn on the cob

b. French fries

● ●

If you picked mostly As—you're a Hamburger.

- You're an easygoing person.

If you picked mostly Bs—you're a Cheeseburger.

- You're a unique-minded individual.

Are You a Muffin or a Cupcake?

1. Do you prefer rain or snow?

   a. Rain

   b. Snow

2. Are you more serious or silly?

   a. Serious

   b. Silly

3. Are you tall or short?

   a. Tall

   b. Short

4. Would you rather live in the countryside or in the city?

   a. In the countryside

   b. In the city

5. Do you prefer the mountains or the ocean?

   a. The mountains

   b. The ocean

6. Do you prefer books or TV?

   a. Books

   b. TV

7. Do you prefer dine-in or delivery?

   a. Dine-in

   b. Delivery

8. Would you rather be amazing at singing or dancing?

a. Singing

b. Dancing

9. Do you prefer toast or bagels?

a. Toast

b. Bagels

10. Do you prefer salty foods or sweet foods?

a. Salty

b. Sweet

• •

If you picked mostly As—you got Muffin.

• You're more low-key and appreciate your alone time.

If you picked mostly Bs—you got Cupcake.

• You're outgoing and full of energy.

Based on the Food Pairs You Pick, Are You More like Blair Waldorf or Serena van der Woodsen from *Gossip Girl*?

1. Which is the better food pair?

  a. Peanut butter and jelly

  b. Ham and cheese

2. Which is the better food pair?

  a. Fries and ice cream

  b. Cake and ice cream

3. Which is the better food pair?

  a. Apples and peanut butter

  b. Apples and caramel

4. Which is the better food pair?

  a. Peanut butter and chocolate

  b. Pretzels and chocolate

5. Which is the better food pair?

  a. Chicken and waffles

  b. Pancakes and bacon

6. Which is the better food pair?

  a. Chips and cheese

  b. Chips and salsa

7. Which is the better food pair?

   a. Burger and fries

   b. Spaghetti and meatballs

8. Which is the better food pair?

   a. Cheese and crackers

   b. Hummus and pita

9. Which is the better food pair?

   a. Bread and butter

   b. Biscuits and gravy

• •

If you picked mostly As—you got Serena van der Woodsen.

If you picked mostly Bs—you got Blair Waldorf.

Based on Your Favorite Fast-Food Restaurants, Are You More like Lilo or Stitch?

1. Which fast-food restaurant do you prefer?

  a. Subway

  b. Jimmy John's

2. Which fast-food restaurant do you prefer?

  a. Sonic

  b. Wendy's

3. Which fast-food restaurant do you prefer?

  a. Steak 'n Shake

  b. Culver's

4. Which fast-food restaurant do you prefer?

  a. Burger King

  b. McDonald's

5. Which fast-food restaurant do you prefer?

  a. In-N-Out Burger

  b. Chick-fil-A

6. Which fast-food restaurant do you prefer?

  a. Kentucky Fried Chicken

  b. Popeyes Louisiana Kitchen

7. Which fast-food restaurant do you prefer?

a. Taco Bell

b. Chipotle Mexican Grill

8. Which fast-food restaurant do you prefer?

a. Jack in the Box

b. Panera Bread

9. Which fast-food restaurant do you prefer?

a. Hardee's

b. Arby's

10. Which fast-food restaurant do you prefer?

a. Pizza Hut

b. Domino's

11. Which fast-food restaurant do you prefer?

a. Whataburger

b. Shake Shack

• •

If you picked mostly As—you got Stitch.

If you picked mostly Bs—you got Lilo.

Are You More Left-Brained or Right-Brained?

1. Would you consider yourself well organized?

   a. Yes

   b. No

2. Do you prefer working alone or with others?

   a. Alone

   b. With others

3. Did you get good grades in school?

   a. Yes

   b. No

4. Are you normally on time to events?

   a. Yes

   b. No

5. Do you get stressed out easily?

   a. Yes

   b. No

6. Would you consider yourself a romantic person?

   a. Not really

   b. Yes

7. Do you prefer math or English?

   a. Math

   b. English

8. Do you like to take risks?

a. Not at all

b. Yes

9. Are you a rule breaker?

a. Of course not

b. Yes

10. Do you gesture with your hands a lot?

a. No

b. Yes

11. Do you find sticking to a schedule to be boring?

a. No

b. It gets boring

12. Do you save your money or spend it?

a. I save it

b. I spend it

13. Are you more shy or outgoing?

a. Shy

b. Outgoing

● ●

If you picked mostly As—you got Left-Brained.

- You're analytical, logical, detail- and fact-oriented, numerical, and likely to think in words.

If you picked mostly Bs—you got Right-Brained.

- You're intuitive, thoughtful, subjective, and likely to think in images.

Are You More Sweet or Salty?

1. Do you prefer Coke or Pepsi?

   a. Coke

   b. Pepsi

2. Do you eat meat?

   a. No

   b. Yes

3. Do you prefer cake or pie?

   a. Cake

   b. Pie

4. Do you prefer chocolate or vanilla?

   a. Chocolate

   b. Vanilla

5. Do you prefer pink or purple?

   a. Pink

   b. Purple

6. Are you more of an introvert or an extrovert?

   a. Introvert

   b. Extrovert

7. Do you prefer romance movies or comedy movies?

   a. Romance

   b. Comedy

8. Do you prefer living in the countryside or in the city?

   a. Countryside

   b. City

9. Do you like watching sports?

   a. No

   b. Yes

10. Do you prefer fruits or vegetables?

   a. Fruits

   b. Vegetables

11. Do you prefer country music or rock music?

   a. Country music

   b. Rock music

12. Do you prefer Facebook or Twitter?

   a. Facebook

   b. Twitter

● ●

If you picked mostly As—you got Sweet.

If you picked mostly Bs—you got Salty.

Are You Pink or Purple?

1. Do you prefer sunrise or sunset?

a. Sunrise

b. Sunset

2. Do you prefer jelly or peanut butter?

a. Jelly

b. Peanut butter

3. Would you rather live in the country or in the city?

a. Country

b. City

4. Which flower do you prefer?

a. Sunflower

b. Rose

5. Would you rather get a gift or give one?

a. Get a gift

b. Give a gift

6. Do you prefer fruits or vegetables?

a. Fruits

b. Vegetables

7. Do you prefer dogs or cats?

a. Dogs

b. Cats

8. Do you prefer Skittles or M&M's?

a. Skittles

b. M&M's

9. Are you afraid of heights?

a. Yes

b. No

10. Which Disney movie do you prefer?

a. *The Lion King*

b. *The Little Mermaid*

• •

If you picked mostly As—you got Pink.

• You're loving, kind, and nurturing.

If you picked mostly Bs—you got Purple.

• You're sensitive, understanding, and supportive.

Are You More like Crunchy Cheetos or Cheetos Puffs?

1. Do you prefer sweet or sour?

   a. Sweet

   b. Sour

2. Are you a daredevil?

   a. No

   b. Yes

3. Do you speak more than one language?

   a. Yes

   b. No

4. Do you prefer movies or TV shows?

   a. Movies

   b. TV shows

5. Do you prefer soccer or football?

   a. Soccer

   b. Football

6. Do you normally stay up late?

   a. No

   b. Yes

7. Do you swear a lot?

   a. No

   b. Yes

8. Which cheesy food is better?

a. Cheesy potatoes

b. Macaroni and cheese

9. Do you believe in ghosts?

a. Yes

b. No

10. Are you good at math?

a. Yes

b. No

11. Do you prefer Instagram or Twitter?

a. Instagram

b. Twitter

12. How do you feel about wearing socks with sandals?

a. It's not cute

b. I like it

13. Would you consider yourself active?

a. Yes

b. No

• •

If you picked mostly As—you got Cheetos Puffs.

- Your personality is soft and gentle.

If you picked mostly Bs—you got Crunchy Cheetos.

- Your personality has a little bit of a crunch to it. You're spunky.

Are You a Land Cow or a Sea Cow?

1. Do you prefer winter or summer?

   a. Winter

   b. Summer

2. Do you prefer fruits or vegetables?

   a. Fruits

   b. Vegetables

3. Do you prefer pasta or pizza?

   a. Pasta

   b. Pizza

4. Do you prefer sweet foods or savory foods?

   a. Sweet

   b. Savory

5. Do you prefer action movies or comedy movies?

   a. Action movies

   b. Comedy movies

6. Do you prefer Netflix or YouTube?

   a. Netflix

   b. YouTube

7. Do you prefer whole wheat bread or white bread?

   a. Whole wheat bread

   b. White bread

8. Do you prefer rock music or country music?

a. Rock music

b. Country music

9. Do you prefer board games or card games?

a. Board games

b. Card games

10. Do you prefer the beach or a lake?

a. The beach

b. A lake

11. Do you prefer cats or dogs?

a. Cats

b. Dogs

12. Do you prefer football or baseball?

a. Football

b. Baseball

• •

If you picked mostly As—you got Sea Cow.

• You're cool and like to stay current with the trends.

If you picked mostly Bs—you got Land Cow.

• You're grounded, and you don't like sticking out in a crowd.

Are You Dora or Boots from Dora the Explorer?

1. How do you pronounce "caramel"?

a. "Care-a-mel"

b. "Car-mull"

2. How do you eat Oreos?

a. Twist them

b. Bite into them

3. Are you organized?

a. Yes

b. No

4. Do you prefer chocolate or vanilla?

a. Chocolate

b. Vanilla

5. Are you afraid of change?

a. No

b. Yes

6. Do you prefer cake or cookies?

a. Cake

b. Cookies

7. Do you prefer M&M's or Skittles?

a. M&M's

b. Skittles

8. Do you speak more than one language?

   a. Yes

   b. No

• •

If you picked mostly As—you're Dora.

If you picked mostly Bs—you're Boots.

Based on the Crazy Sandwich You Create, Are You More like Phineas Flynn or Ferb Fletcher in *Phineas and Ferb*?

1. Choose a bread:

  a. Whole wheat

  b. White

  c. Rye

  d. Italian

2. Put something on your sandwich:

  a. Tomatoes

  b. Sliced turkey

  c. Mayonnaise

  d. Peanut butter

3. Put something on your sandwich:

  a. Jelly

  b. Sliced ham

  c. Pepperoni

  d. Sliced cheese

4. Put something on your sandwich:

  a. Balsamic vinaigrette

  b. Bacon

  c. Lettuce

  d. Sliced chicken

5. Put something weird on your sandwich:

a. Baked beans

b. Chocolate sauce

c. Marshmallow Fluff

d. Potato chips

6. Do you want your sandwich toasted?

a. No

b. Yes, I want it crunchy

c. Maybe a little

d. I don't really have a preference

● ●

If you picked mostly As and Cs—you got Ferb Fletcher.

If you picked mostly Bs and Ds—you got Phineas Flynn.

Based on the Macaroni and Cheese You Choose, Are You Outgoing or Reserved?

1. Choose a macaroni and cheese:

a. Shells and cheese

b. Cavatappi macaroni and cheese

2. Choose a macaroni and cheese:

a. Bacon macaroni and cheese

b. Spinach macaroni and cheese

3. Choose a macaroni and cheese:

a. Kraft Macaroni and Cheese

b. Kraft Shaped Macaroni and Cheese

4. Choose a macaroni and cheese:

a. White macaroni and cheese

b. Jalapeño macaroni and cheese

5. Choose a macaroni and cheese:

a. Regular macaroni and cheese

b. Baked macaroni and cheese

6. Choose a macaroni and cheese:

a. Macaroni and cheese bites

b. Caribbean macaroni and cheese pie

7. Choose a macaroni and cheese:

a. Macaroni and cheese pizza

b. Macaroni and cheese burger

8. Choose a macaroni and cheese:

a. Green pea macaroni and cheese

b. Spinach artichoke macaroni and cheese

• •

If you picked mostly As—you got Reserved.

If you picked mostly Bs—you got Outgoing.

Are You More like Mickey Mouse or Minnie Mouse?

1. **Which movie genre do you prefer?**

   a. Action

   b. Comedy

2. **Which candy do you prefer?**

   a. Reese's Peanut Butter Cups

   b. SweeTarts

3. **Do you prefer warm or cool colors?**

   a. Warm colors

   b. Cool colors

4. **Do you prefer cheese popcorn or caramel popcorn?**

   a. Cheese popcorn

   b. Caramel popcorn

5. **Would you rather drive a truck or an SUV?**

   a. Truck

   b. SUV

6. **Do you prefer Xbox or Wii?**

   a. Xbox

   b. Wii

7. **Would you rather be good at cooking or at baking?**

   a. Cooking

   b. Baking

8. Do you prefer YouTube or Netflix?

a. YouTube

b. Netflix

9. Do you prefer soft pretzels or hard pretzels?

a. Soft pretzels

b. Hard pretzels

10. Do you look younger or older than your actual age?

a. Younger

b. Older

11. Do you prefer salty foods or sweet foods?

a. Salty foods

b. Sweet foods

12. Which animated movie do you prefer?

a. *Monsters, Inc.*

b. *Wreck-It Ralph*

• •

If you picked mostly As—you got Mickey Mouse.

If you picked mostly Bs—you got Minnie Mouse.

Are You More like Mario or Luigi in the game Super Mario Bros.?

1. Do you prefer waffles or pancakes?

a. Waffles

b. Pancakes

2. Have you ever broken a bone?

a. No

b. Yes

3. Do you believe in ghosts?

a. Yes

b. No

4. Which word describes you best?

a. Competitive

b. Confident

5. Which Wii game is better?

a. Super Mario Bros.

b. Mario Kart

6. Would you rather live without music or without TV?

a. Without music

b. Without TV

7. Would you rather have ten sisters or ten brothers?

a. Ten sisters

b. Ten brothers

8. Do you prefer Princess Daisy or Princess Peach?

a. Princess Daisy

b. Princess Peach

9. Do you prefer Yoshi or Toad?

a. Yoshi

b. Toad

10. Choose a cartoon character:

a. Sandy Cheeks from *SpongeBob SquarePants*

b. Bugs Bunny from *Looney Tunes*

11. Do you prefer pasta or pizza?

a. Pasta

b. Pizza

12. Do you like roller coasters?

a. No

b. Yes

13. Choose a fast-food restaurant:

a. Burger King

b. McDonald's

• •

If you picked mostly As—you got Luigi.

If you picked mostly Bs—you got Mario.

Are You a Taco or a Quesadilla?

1. **Do you prefer popcorn or Popsicles?**

   a. Popcorn

   b. Popsicles

2. **Would you rather spend time with puppies or kittens?**

   a. Puppies

   b. Kittens

3. **Do you prefer pancakes or waffles?**

   a. Pancakes

   b. Waffles

4. **Do you prefer Facebook or Twitter?**

   a. Facebook

   b. Twitter

5. **Do you prefer *Star Wars* or *Harry Potter*?**

   a. *Star Wars*

   b. *Harry Potter*

6. **Would you rather go to Disney World or Disneyland?**

   a. Disney World

   b. Disneyland

7. **Do you prefer peanut butter or Nutella?**

   a. Peanut butter

   b. Nutella

8. Do you prefer chicken nuggets or chicken fingers?

a. Chicken nuggets

b. Chicken fingers

• •

If you picked mostly As—you got Taco.

- You're very straightforward.

If you picked mostly Bs—you got Quesadilla.

- You enjoy stepping out of your comfort zone and trying new things.

Are You Beans on Toast or Bread and Butter?

1. Do you prefer peanut butter or jelly?

a. Peanut butter

b. Jelly

2. Do you prefer dogs or cats?

a. Dogs

b. Cats

3. Do you prefer the beach or a water park?

a. Beach

b. Waterpark

4. Do you prefer muffins or croissants?

a. Muffins

b. Croissants

5. Would you rather own a private plane or a private yacht?

a. Private plane

b. Private yacht

6. Do you prefer lemonade or iced tea?

a. Lemonade

b. Iced tea

7. Do you prefer salad or soup?

a. Salad

b. Soup

8. Do you prefer apples or pineapples?

a. Apples

b. Pineapples

9. Do you prefer pepperoni or peppers on your pizza?

a. Pepperoni

b. Peppers

10. Where would you rather go on vacation?

a. France

b. Ireland

11. Do you prefer Jell-O parfait or pudding?

a. Parfait

b. Pudding

• •

If you picked mostly As—you got Bread and Butter.

• You're sarcastic and simple.

If you picked mostly Bs—you got Beans on Toast.

• You're sophisticated and apologetic.

Are You Cheese or Cake?

1. Do you prefer Justin Bieber or Justin Timberlake?

  a. Justin Bieber

  b. Justin Timberlake

2. Do you prefer cheddar cheese or Parmesan?

  a. Cheddar cheese

  b. Parmesan

3. Do you prefer movies or books?

  a. Movies

  b. Books

4. Do you prefer breakfast or dinner?

  a. Breakfast

  b. Dinner

5. Do you prefer cinnamon coffee cake or angel food cake?

  a. Cinnamon coffee cake

  b. Angel food cake

6. Do you prefer pop music or rock music?

  a. Pop music

  b. Rock music

7. Do you prefer a scooter or a bicycle?

  a. A scooter

  b. A bicycle

8. Do you prefer whipped cream or marshmallows?

a. Whipped cream

b. Marshmallows

• •

If you picked mostly As—you got Cake.

• People love every layer of you.

If you picked mostly Bs—you got Cheese.

• People say you make such a Gouda friend.

Are You Salsa the Dance or Salsa the Food?

1. What time do you normally wake up?

  a. After 9 a.m.

  b. Before 9 a.m.

2. How would you describe yourself?

  a. Chill

  b. Ambitious

3. If you could be an animal for the day, which would you choose?

  a. A dog

  b. A monkey

4. Which style of dance do you prefer?

  a. Hip-hop

  b. Jazz

5. Which music genre do you prefer?

  a. Rap

  b. Country

6. What's something you can't live without?

  a. Sweatpants

  b. Chocolate

7. What's something you think you're bad at?

   a. Saving money

   b. Staying focused

8. Choose a red food:

   a. Red velvet cake

   b. Cherries

9. Choose a dip:

   a. Guacamole

   b. Queso

10. Which color do you prefer?

   a. Red

   b. Blue

● ●

If you picked mostly As—you got Salsa the Food.

   • You're social and reasonable.

If you picked mostly Bs—you got Salsa the Dance.

   • You're well coordinated and energetic.

Are You a Doughnut or a Doughnut Hole?

1. Choose a hobby to take up:

  a. Magic

  b. Dancing

  c. Baking

  d. Photography

2. Choose a drink to have with some doughnuts:

  a. Smoothie

  b. Water

  c. Milk

  d. Juice

3. Choose a doughnut flavor:

  a. Vanilla frosted with sprinkles

  b. Powdered

  c. Chocolate glaze

  d. Sour cream

4. Choose a type of nuts:

  a. Almonds

  b. Peanuts

  c. Cashews

  d. Pecans

5. Choose a word to describe yourself:

a. Nutty

b. Bland

c. Sweet

d. Bitter

6. Choose some sprinkles:

a. Confetti

b. Rainbow

c. Chocolate

d. Edible glitter

7. Choose a round food:

a. Popcorn balls

b. Meatballs

c. Cookie dough balls

d. Cheese balls

8. Choose a place to eat some doughnuts:

a. On a boat

b. In bed

c. By the beach

d. On a mountaintop

• •

If you picked mostly As and Ds—you got Doughnut Hole.

- In one word: you're courageous.

If you picked mostly Bs and Cs—you got Doughnut.

- In one word: you're frank.

Are You Rainbow Sprinkles or Chocolate Sprinkles?

1. Do you prefer music or sports?

   a. Music

   b. Sports

2. Are you a night owl or an early bird?

   a. Night owl

   b. Early bird

3. Do you prefer vanilla or chocolate?

   a. Vanilla

   b. Chocolate

4. Are you an extrovert or an introvert?

   a. Extrovert

   b. Introvert

5. Do you prefer salty or sweet foods?

   a. Salty

   b. Sweet

6. Do you prefer French fries or breadsticks?

   a. French fries

   b. Breadsticks

7. Which is more important to you?

   a. Friends

   b. Family

8. Which city would you rather live in?

a. Los Angeles

b. New York City

9. Do you get annoyed easily?

a. No

b. Yes

10. Do you prefer Skittles or M&M's?

a. Skittles

b. M&M's

• •

If you picked mostly As—you got Rainbow Sprinkles.

• Your personality is colorful, and you're free-spirited.

If you picked mostly Bs—you got Chocolate Sprinkles.

• Your personality is rational, and you're more of a reserved person.

Based on the Sliced Foods You Pick, Are You Shrek or Donkey?

1. Pick a sliced food:

   a. Ham

   b. Bread

2. Pick a sliced food:

   a. Lasagna

   b. Pizza

3. Pick a sliced food:

   a. Cake

   b. Pie

4. Pick a sliced food:

   a. Bagel

   b. Cheesecake

5. Pick a sliced food:

   a. Cheese

   b. Bacon

6. Pick a sliced food:

   a. Watermelon

   b. Apple

7. Pick a sliced food:

   a. Corn bread

   b. Meat loaf

8. Pick a sliced food:

a. Sausage

b. Potatoes

9. Pick a sliced food:

a. Avocado

b. Cucumber

10. Pick a sliced food:

a. Frittata

b. French toast

• •

If you picked mostly As—you got Donkey.

If you picked mostly Bs—you got Shrek.

Are You a Lime or a Lemon?

1. **Do you prefer to hang out with friends in town or at home?**
   a. In town
   b. At home

2. **Do you prefer babies or dogs?**
   a. Babies
   b. Dogs

3. **Do you prefer Twitter or YouTube?**
   a. Twitter
   b. YouTube

4. **Do you prefer the aquarium or the zoo?**
   a. Aquarium
   b. Zoo

5. **Do you prefer sunflowers or roses?**
   a. Sunflowers
   b. Roses

6. **Do you prefer a car or a truck?**
   a. Car
   b. Truck

7. Do you prefer guitar or piano?

a. Guitar

b. Piano

8. Do you prefer sneakers or flip-flops?

a. Sneakers

b. Flip-flops

9. Do you prefer tattoos or piercings?

a. Tattoos

b. Piercings

• •

If you picked mostly As—you got Lemon.

• You're sour and inventive.

If you picked mostly Bs—you got Lime.

• You're bitter and intuitive.

Based on Your Cookie Preferences, Are You More like a Unicorn or a Narwhal?

1. Choose a cookie:
   a. Butter cookie
   b. Fortune cookie

2. Choose a cookie:
   a. Chocolate chip cookie
   b. Sugar cookie

3. Choose a cookie:
   a. Gingerbread cookie
   b. Macaron

4. Choose a cookie:
   a. Peanut butter cookie
   b. Snickerdoodle

5. Choose a cookie:
   a. Oatmeal raisin cookie
   b. Shortbread cookie

6. Choose a cookie:
   a. Macadamia nut cookie
   b. M&M's cookie

7. Choose a cookie:

   a. Thumbprint cookie

   b. Snowball cookie

8. Choose a cookie:

   a. Peanut butter chocolate chip cookie

   b. Frosted sugar cookie

• •

If you picked mostly As—you got Narwhal.

   • You like to stick with what you know.

If you picked mostly Bs—you got Unicorn.

   • Stepping out of your comfort zone is something you enjoy and don't fear.

Are You the Sun or the Moon?

1. Do you like roller coasters?

   a. No

   b. Yes

2. Do you prefer whole wheat bread or white bread?

   a. Whole wheat bread

   b. White bread

3. Do you prefer blue or pink?

   a. Blue

   b. Pink

4. Do you drink milk?

   a. No

   b. Yes

5. Do you prefer escalators or elevators?

   a. Escalators

   b. Elevators

6. Are you a good liar?

   a. Yes

   b. No

7. Do you prefer pudding or yogurt?

   a. Pudding

   b. Yogurt

8. Do you like spicy foods?

   a. No

   b. Yes

9. Would you consider yourself creative?

   a. No

   b. Yes

• •

If you picked mostly As—you got the Moon.

   • You're great at controlling your emotions, and you value your alone time.

If you picked mostly Bs—you got the Sun.

   • You're well rounded and bright.

5

Who Am I?

Which of the Jonas Brothers Are You?

1. Choose a color:
   a. Blue

   b. Red

   c. Green

2. Choose a milkshake flavor:
   a. Vanilla

   b. Strawberry

   c. Chocolate

3. Choose a city:
   a. Paris

   b. Miami

   c. Los Angeles

4. Choose a music genre:
   a. Country

   b. Rock

   c. Pop

5. Choose a breakfast food:
   a. Waffles

   b. Pancakes

   c. French toast   *Continued*

6. Choose a pet:

a. Dog

b. Turtle

c. Cat

7. Choose a snack:

a. Goldfish crackers

b. Granola bar

c. Peanut butter–filled pretzels

8. Choose a female celebrity:

a. Rihanna

b. Natalie Portman

c. Ariana Grande

9. Choose somewhere to live:

a. In the country

b. On the beach

c. In a city

10. Choose a drink:

a. Coffee

b. Lemonade

c. Pop

11. Choose a candy:

a. Kit Kat

b. Tootsie Roll

c. Sour Skittles

12. Choose a Jonas Brothers song:

a. "Lovebug"

b. "S.O.S."

c. "Burnin' Up"

• •

If you picked mostly As—you got Nick Jonas.

If you picked mostly Bs—you got Kevin Jonas.

If you picked mostly Cs—you got Joe Jonas.

What Kind of Smoothie Are You?

⋆✰⋆✰⋆✰⋆✰⋆✰⋆✰⋆✰⋆✰⋆✰⋆✰⋆✰⋆✰⋆✰⋆✰⋆✰⋆

1. Choose a smoothie place:
a. Jamba Juice

b. Orange Julius

c. Tropical Smoothie Cafe

d. Surf City Squeeze

2. Choose a color:
a. Gray

b. Coral

c. Pink

d. Purple

3. Choose a hobby:
a. Photography

b. Dance

c. Baking

d. Playing video games

4. Choose a fruit:
a. Blackberries

b. Avocado

c. Watermelon

d. Blueberries

5. Choose a veggie:
a. Red pepper

b. Onion

c. Celery

d. Carrot

6. Choose a breakfast item:

a. Cereal

b. Scrambled eggs

c. Oatmeal

d. Pancakes

7. Which is the best time for a smoothie?

a. At night

b. After working out

c. For breakfast

d. Anytime

• •

If you picked mostly As—you got Black Raspberry Smoothie.

- You're independent and strong. You don't let anyone mess with you. But you're also a little stubborn.

If you picked mostly Bs—you got Mango Orange Smoothie.

- You're hilarious and never like to take things too seriously.

If you picked mostly Cs—you got Strawberry Banana Smoothie.

- You're sweet and selfless, and you love to be around other people.

If you picked mostly Ds—you got Piña Colada Smoothie.

- You're all about fun!

Which Classic Holiday Candy Are You?

★ ★

1. Choose something to be talented at:

a. School

b. Art

c. Sports

2. Which of the following candies is the worst?

a. Gumdrops

b. Circus peanuts

c. Hard caramels

3. Choose a wacky holiday:

a. Wiggle Your Toes Day

b. Humiliation Day

c. Bean Day

4. What is your current relationship status?

a. Taken

b. Single

c. It's complicated

5. Choose a holiday food:

a. Gingerbread cookies

b. Easter ham

c. Thanksgiving stuffing

6. Do you prefer dogs or cats?

a. Dogs

b. I can't choose!

c. Cats

7. Choose a comfort food:

a. Soup

b. Ice cream

c. Mashed potatoes

8. Choose someone to spend the holidays with:

a. Your friends

b. Your significant other

c. Your pet

• •

If you picked mostly As—you got Conversation Hearts.

- You're supersweet and have a very colorful personality. People come to you for words of advice or just a pick-me-up every once in a while.

If you picked mostly Bs—you got Candy Cane.

- You're a refreshing, light presence in your friends' lives. You're incredibly sweet, and you find a way to leave your mark wherever you go.

If you picked mostly Cs—you got Candy Corn.

- You're a very polarizing person. Some people *love* you and some people just . . . don't. Hey, that's life! The people who love you are loyal for life; you're surrounded by many great friends.

What Type of Chicken Nugget Are You?

****

1. Pick a word to describe yourself:
- a. Funny
- b. Sassy
- c. Knowledgeable

2. Pick a condiment for chicken nuggets:
- a. Ranch dressing
- b. Honey mustard
- c. Ketchup

3. Pick a type of fries to eat with chicken nuggets:
- a. Smiley face fries
- b. Curly fries
- c. Skinny-cut fries

4. Pick a career:
- a. YouTuber
- b. Movie director
- c. Doctor/nurse

5. Pick another chicken-based food:
- a. Chicken quesadilla
- b. Barbecue chicken pizza
- c. Chicken pot pie

6. **Which one of these restaurants has the best chicken nuggets?**

    a. Chick-fil-A

    b. Wendy's

    c. McDonald's

• •

If you picked mostly As—you got Dinosaur Chicken Nugget.

    • Life is all fun and games to you.

If you picked mostly Bs—you got Spicy Chicken Nugget.

    • You're spunky and gutsy.

If you picked mostly Cs—you got Traditional Chicken Nugget.

    • You focus on the essentials of life.

Based on the Bread You Choose, Which Disney Prince Are You?

★ ★

1. Choose a bread:

a. Panettone

b. Flatbread

c. Cinnamon raisin

d. Croutons

2. Choose a bread:

a. Ciabatta

b. Corn bread

c. Toast

d. Dinner roll

3. Choose a bread:

a. Multigrain

b. Garlic

c. Crumpet

d. Bagel

4. Choose a bread:

a. Brioche loaf

b. Biscuit

c. White

d. Rye

5. Choose a bread:

a. Naan

b. Breadsticks

c. Sourdough

d. Baguette

6. Choose a bread:

a. Pita

b. Cinnamon monkey

c. Banana

d. Whole wheat

• •

If you picked mostly As—you got Prince Charming from *Cinderella*.

If you picked mostly Bs—you got the Beast from *Beauty and the Beast*.

If you picked mostly Cs—you got Prince Naveen from *The Princess and the Frog*.

If you picked mostly Ds—you got Flynn Rider from *Tangled*.

Which Pop-Tarts Flavor Are You?

1. Choose a movie:

   a. *Girls Trip*

   b. *The Benchwarmers*

   c. *Wedding Crashers*

   d. *Bridesmaids*

   e. *21 Jump Street*

   f. *Anchorman: The Legend of Ron Burgundy*

2. Choose an ice cream flavor:

   a. Chocolate

   b. Birthday cake

   c. Vanilla

   d. Strawberry

   e. Raspberry swirl

   f. Butter pecan

3. Choose a word to describe yourself:

   a. Fearless

   b. Happy

   c. Competitive

   d. Caring

   e. Energetic

   f. Chill

4. Choose a fruit:

a. Watermelon

b. Banana

c. Blueberries

d. Strawberries

e. Raspberries

f. Apple

5. Choose a snack:

a. Granola bar

b. Yogurt

c. Peanuts

d. Apple and peanut butter

e. Chips

f. Goldfish crackers

6. Choose a sport:

a. Snowboarding

b. Gymnastics

c. Basketball

d. Soccer

e. Hockey

f. Baseball

7. Choose a beverage:

a. Chocolate milk

b. Strawberry milkshake

c. Berry smoothie

d. Coffee

e. Pop

f. Lemonade   *Continued*

8. Choose a vacation:

a. Taking a road trip to Yellowstone National Park

b. Exploring Hawaii

c. Going on an Alaskan cruise

d. Sightseeing in Paris

e. Partying it up in Las Vegas

f. Relaxing on the beach in Turks and Caicos

• •

If you picked mostly As—you got S'mores.

- You're all about the outdoors and spending time with the people you care about.

If you picked mostly Bs—you got Confetti Cupcake.

- You're very upbeat and are filled with lots of energy.

If you picked mostly Cs—you got Blueberry.

- You can be reserved at times, but your close friends really know how funny and kind you are.

If you picked mostly Ds—you got Strawberry.

- You're as sweet as can be. You love to help others in any way you can.

If you picked mostly Es—you got Wildlicious Wild! Berry.

- It's in the name! You're wild and crazy. You enjoy showing everyone you mean a good time!

If you picked mostly Fs—you got Brown Sugar Cinnamon.

- You're all about me time, and you hate being told what to do.

Which Kind of French Fries Are You?

★ ★ ★ ★ ★★ ★ ★ ★ ★ ★ ★ ★★ ★ ★ ★ ★ ★ ★ ★ ★★ ★ ★ ★ ★ ★ ★ ★ ★★ ★ ★ ★ ★ ★ ★ ★★

1. Choose a drink:

- a. Lemonade
- b. Water
- c. Beer
- d. Pop
- e. Kool-Aid
- f. Milk
- g. Orange juice

2. Choose a sport to watch:

- a. Basketball
- b. Soccer
- c. Football
- d. Golf
- e. Gymnastics
- f. Nascar racing
- g. Volleyball

3. Choose some candy:

- a. Sour Patch Kids
- b. Hershey's Kisses Milk Chocolate
- c. Kit Kat
- d. Tootsie Roll
- e. Gummy bears
- f. Starbursts
- g. Skittles

Continued

4. Choose a school subject:

  a. Yearbook

  b. English

  c. Gym

  d. Home economics

  e. Art

  f. History

  g. Science

5. Choose a fair food:

  a. Deep-fried Oreos

  b. Popcorn

  c. Corn dog

  d. Funnel cake

  e. Cotton candy

  f. Churros

  g. Elephant ear

6. Choose a TV show:

  a. *Stranger Things*

  b. *Full House*

  c. *The Walking Dead*

  d. *Shameless*

  e. *Modern Family*

  f. *Superstore*

  g. *Game of Thrones*

7. Choose a pasta:

  a. Penne with vodka sauce

  b. Spaghetti

c. Lasagna

d. Fettuccine Alfredo

e. Macaroni and cheese

f. Buttered noodles

g. Ravioli

• •

If you picked mostly As—you got Curly Fries.

• In one word: you're distinguished.

If you picked mostly Bs—you got Standard-Cut Fries.

• In one word: you're straightforward.

If you picked mostly Cs—you got Steak-Cut Fries.

• In one word: you're skilled.

If you picked mostly Ds—you got Waffle Fries.

• In one word: you're silly.

If you picked mostly Es—you got Smiley Face Fries.

• In one word: you're cheerful.

If you picked mostly Fs—you got Crinkle-Cut Fries.

• In one word: you're memorable.

If you picked mostly Gs—you got Tater Tots.

• In one word: you're powerful.

Based on the Fast-Food Items You Select, Which *SpongeBob SquarePants* Character Are You?

1. Pick something from McDonald's:

   a. Hash browns

   b. Big Mac

   c. French fries

   d. Hamburger

   e. Chicken nuggets

2. Pick something from Wendy's:

   a. Taco salad

   b. Frosty

   c. Chili

   d. Chicken nuggets

   e. French fries

3. Pick something from Taco Bell:

   a. Cheesy Bean and Rice Burrito

   b. Nacho fries

   c. Crunchy taco

   d. Soft taco

   e. Cheese quesadilla

4. Pick something from Kentucky Fried Chicken:

   a. Biscuits

   b. Extra Crispy chicken

   c. Potato wedges

   d. Smoky Mountain BBQ Sandwich

   e. Popcorn Nuggets

5. Pick something from Burger King:

   a. Sausage, Egg & Cheese Biscuit

   b. Chicken Fries

   c. Crispy Chicken sandwich

   d. Bacon Double Cheeseburger

   e. Onion rings

6. Pick something from Subway:

   a. Veggie Delight Sub

   b. Meatball Marinara Sub

   c. Italian BMT Sub

   d. Turkey Breast Sub

   e. Bag of chips

• •

If you picked mostly As—you got Squidward Q. Tentacles.

If you picked mostly Bs—you got Patrick Star.

If you picked mostly Cs—you got Mr. Krabs.

If you picked mostly Ds—you got SpongeBob SquarePants.

If you picked mostly Es—you got Sheldon J. Plankton.

Based on Your Favorite Food, Which Underrated Disney Character Are You?

1. Choose a doughnut:

a. Powdered

b. Cinnamon roll

c. Chocolate frosted

d. Glazed

e. Cinnamon sugar

f. Blueberry cake

2. Choose a meat:

a. Bacon

b. Ham

c. Roast beef

d. Turkey

e. Chicken

f. I don't like meat

3. Choose a cake flavor:

a. Strawberry

b. Chocolate

c. Lemon

d. Funfetti

e. Vanilla

f. Red velvet

4. Choose a fruit:

a. Apple

b. Watermelon

c. Orange

d. Blueberries

e. Strawberries

f. Banana

5. Choose a cheesy food:

a. Nachos

b. Grilled cheese

c. Mozzarella sticks

d. Cheeseburger

e. Garlic bread

f. Cheesy potatoes

6. Choose a pizza topping:

a. Just cheese

b. Pineapple

c. Sausage

d. Mushrooms

e. Pepperoni

f. Green peppers

7. Choose a snack:

a. Cheese sticks

b. Pretzels

c. Popcorn

d. Oreos

e. Pizza bagels

f. Yogurt

Continued

8. Choose a frozen treat:

  a. Frozen yogurt

  b. Sherbet

  c. Ice cream cake

  d. Fudge Popsicle

  e. Milkshake

  f. Ice cream sandwich

• •

If you picked mostly As—you got Sergeant Tibbs from *101 Dalmatians*.

If you picked mostly Bs—you got Dopey from *Snow White and the Seven Dwarfs*.

If you picked mostly Cs—you got Zazu from *The Lion King*.

If you picked mostly Ds—you got Meeko from *Pocahontas*.

If you picked mostly Es—you got Scuttle from *The Little Mermaid*.

If you picked mostly Fs—you got Nana from *Peter Pan*.

Based on the Tropical Vacation You Plan, Which Aquatic Animal Are You?

★☆★★★☆★★★★☆★★★★★☆★★★★★☆★★★☆★★★★☆★★★★★☆★★★☆★★★★☆

1. Who will be going on vacation with you?

a. Your family

b. Your pet

c. Your close friends

d. Just you

2. Where will you be going?

a. Maldives

b. Hawaii

c. Fiji

d. Bora Bora

3. How long will you be staying?

a. Five days

b. Ten days

c. A month

d. As long as possible!

4. Choose a way to get around once you're there:

a. On a bike

b. On foot

c. In a jeep

d. Whatever you find

Continued

5. Choose a drink to sip on:

a. Smoothie

b. Bahama Mama

c. Lemonade

d. Piña colada

6. Choose an activity to do:

a. Paddleboarding

b. Snorkeling

c. Relaxing on the beach

d. Parasailing

7. Choose another activity to do:

a. Exploring

b. Jet skiing

c. Lying in a hammock

d. Swimming with dolphins

8. Choose one more activity:

a. Zip-lining

b. Partying

c. Shopping

d. Swimming with stingrays

9. Choose a snack to eat:

a. Yogurt and granola

b. Ice cream cone

c. Fresh fruit

d. Slushie

10. **What will be the most exciting thing that happens during your trip?**

   a. You'll get lost while exploring

   b. You'll get really drunk

   c. You'll fall in love

   d. You'll go shark-cage diving

• •

If you picked mostly As—you got Manatee.

   • You're gentle, peaceful, and tend to look toward human activity in search of warmth.

If you picked mostly Bs—you got Sea Lion.

   • You're charming, energetic, and you have an eagerness to your spirit that's irresistibly compelling.

If you picked mostly Cs—you got Dolphin.

   • You're very social and intelligent.

If you picked mostly Ds—you got Jellyfish.

   • You're overachieving, ambitious, and friendly, yet firm.

Which Candy Bar Are You?

★☆★☆★★☆★★☆★★☆★★★☆★★★☆★★★★☆★★★☆★★★☆★★★☆★★★☆★★★★

1. Which of these words best describes you?

   a. Driven

   b. Casual

   c. Energetic

   d. Unique

2. Which of these is your favorite animal?

   a. Tiger

   b. Dog

   c. Goat

   d. Turtle

3. Which of these is your favorite pasta dish?

   a. I don't like pasta

   b. Spaghetti and meatballs

   c. Macaroni and cheese

   d. Lasagna

4. Which of these is your favorite social media platform?

   a. Instagram

   b. Facebook

   c. Snapchat

   d. YouTube

246

5. Which of these is your favorite kind of potatoes?

a. Mashed potatoes

b. French fries

c. Hash browns

d. Potato chips

6. Which of these is your favorite color?

a. Maroon

b. Black

c. Orange

d. Blue

7. Who is your favorite child from *Willy Wonka and the Chocolate Factory?*

a. Veruca Salt

b. Charlie Bucket

c. Mike Teavee

d. Augustus Gloop

8. Which of these is your favorite movie series?

a. *Pirates of the Caribbean*

b. *Harry Potter*

c. *Toy Story*

d. *The Hunger Games*

9. Which of these is your favorite ice cream flavor?

a. Butter pecan

b. Chocolate

c. Mint chocolate chip

d. Chocolate chip cookie dough   *Continued*

10. Which of these is your favorite sport?

   a. Football

   b. Baseball

   c. Basketball

   d. Hockey

• •

If you picked mostly As—you got 100 Grand.

   • You're very motivated, whether it be in terms of money or something else.

If you picked mostly Bs—you got Hershey's Bar.

   • You like to keep life as simple as you possibly can.

If you picked mostly Cs—you got Kit Kat.

   • You're active and prefer to stay busy.

If you picked mostly Ds—you got Nestlé Crunch.

   • You have particular taste when it comes to most things, and you trust your own opinion more than anyone else's.

Which Planet Are You?

1. Choose a pastry:

    a. Cinnamon roll

    b. Macaron

    c. Cream puff

    d. Jelly doughnut

    e. Éclair

2. Choose a fruit or vegetable:

    a. Apple

    b. Grapes

    c. Carrot

    d. Corn

    e. Banana

3. Choose a salty food:

    a. French fries

    b. Pretzel sticks

    c. Tortilla chips

    d. Cashews

    e. Chex Mix

4. Choose a food duo:

    a. Peanut butter and jelly sandwich

    b. Bacon and eggs

    c. Chicken and waffles

Continued

d. Spaghetti and meatballs

e. Macaroni and cheese

5. Choose a sweet food:

a. Vanilla cupcake

b. Brownie

c. S'mores

d. Caramel apple

e. Pancakes with syrup

6. Choose a bread:

a. Baguette

b. Banana bread

c. Biscuits

d. Bagels

e. Breadsticks

• •

If you picked mostly As—you got Earth.

• You're lively and well rounded.

If you picked mostly Bs—you got Mercury.

• You're intellectual and social.

If you picked mostly Cs—you got Mars.

• You're all about desire, action, and energy.

If you picked mostly Ds—you got Saturn.

• You value responsibility and obligation.

If you picked mostly Es—you got Jupiter.

• You're optimistic and understanding.

Which Type of Flower Are You?

★ ★

1. Choose a color:

   a. Pink

   b. Orange

   c. Purple

   d. Lime green

   e. Yellow

   f. Red

2. Choose a dog breed:

   a. Australian shepherd

   b. Golden retriever

   c. Cocker spaniel

   d. Corgi

   e. Yorkshire terrier

   f. German shepherd

3. Choose a food:

   a. Strawberry shortcake

   b. Crackers

   c. Popcorn

   d. Chocolate chip cookies

   e. Waffles

   f. Potato chips

Continued

4. Choose a salty and sweet food combination:

a. Chocolate peanut butter pretzel bites

b. Bacon pineapple bites

c. Caramel corn

d. Chicken and waffles

e. Fries and ice cream

f. Chocolate-covered bacon

5. Choose a flavor of gum:

a. Stride Sour Patch Kids Redberry

b. Orbit Wintermint

c. Hubba Bubba Bubble Tape

d. Extra Sweet Watermelon

e. Trident Tropical Twist

f. 5 Peppermint Cobalt

6. Choose a cereal:

a. Cinnamon Toast Crunch

b. Honeycomb

c. Cap'n Crunch's Crunch Berries

d. Lucky Charms

e. Froot Loops

f. Trix

7. Choose a throwback song:

a. "Beautiful Girls" by Sean Kingston

b. "Waterfalls" by TLC

c. "All Star" by Smash Mouth

d. "Billie Jean" by Michael Jackson

e. "Hollaback Girl" by Gwen Stefani

f. "It Wasn't Me" by Shaggy

8. Choose a TV series:

a. *The Bachelorette*

b. *Grey's Anatomy*

c. *America's Got Talent*

d. *Modern Family*

e. *Friends*

f. *Saturday Night Live*

● ●

If you picked mostly As—you got Rose.

- You're sophisticated and passionate.

If you picked mostly Bs—you got Hydrangea.

- You have great versatility and a great presence.

If you picked mostly Cs—you got Tulip.

- You're positive and laid back and have tons of friends.

If you picked mostly Ds—you got Sweet Pea.

- You live in the moment.

If you picked mostly Es—you got Sunflower.

- You enjoy a life of luxury.

If you picked mostly Fs—you got Snapdragon.

- You're commanding and strong.

Which *Clueless* Character and *Mean Girls* Character Are You a Combo Of?

1. Choose a breakfast food:
a. Cinnamon French toast sticks

b. Granola bar

c. Stack of waffles

d. Scrambled eggs

2. Choose a store:
a. Macy's

b. Nordstrom Rack

c. Target

d. H&M

3. Choose a type of salad:
a. Pasta salad

b. Caesar salad

c. Potato salad

d. Fruit salad

4. Choose a school subject:
a. English

b. History

c. Science

d. Speech

5. Choose a pet:
a. Hamster

b. Fish

   c. Dog

   d. Cat

6. Choose an accessory:

   a. Necklace

   b. Earrings

   c. Rings

   d. Bracelet

7. Choose a city:

   a. New York City

   b. Los Angeles

   c. London

   d. Paris

8. Choose a teen movie:

   a. *17 Again*

   b. *Bring It On*

   c. *The Princess Diaries*

   d. *10 Things I Hate About You*

• •

If you picked mostly As—you got Christian Stovitz from *Clueless* and Karen Smith from *Mean Girls*.

If you picked mostly Bs—you got Dionne Davenport from *Clueless* and Regina George from *Mean Girls*.

If you picked mostly Cs—you got Tai Frasier from *Clueless* and Damian Leigh from *Mean Girls*.

If you picked mostly Ds—you got Cher Horowitz from *Clueless* and Gretchen Wiens from *Mean Girls*.

Which Baby Animal Are You?

* *

1. Choose a pastry:

   a. Cinnamon roll

   b. Muffin

   c. Bagel

   d. Croissant

2. Choose a cheese:

   a. Cheddar

   b. Mozzarella

   c. Colby

   d. Parmesan

3. Choose a fruit:

   a. Grapes

   b. Apple

   c. Banana

   d. Blueberries

4. Choose a sandwich:

   a. Sloppy joe

   b. BLT

   c. Grilled cheese

   d. Peanut butter

5. Choose some cereal:

   a. Cocoa Pebbles

   b. Froot Loops

c. Cinnamon Toast Crunch

d. Apple Jacks

6. Choose a frozen treat:

a. Popsicle

b. Ice cream sandwich

c. Caramel ice cream sundae

d. Sherbet

7. Choose a meat:

a. Chicken

b. Turkey

c. Bacon

d. I don't like meat

8. Choose a type of pizza:

a. Hawaiian

b. Meat lover's

c. Pepperoni

d. Cheese

• •

If you picked mostly As—you got Baby Elephant.

  • You're extroverted and open to new things.

If you picked mostly Bs—you got Baby Goat.

  • You're fun, creative, and definitely sympathetic.

If you picked mostly Cs—you got Baby Panda.

  • You're gentle yet strong.

If you picked mostly Ds—you got Chick.

  • You're social and curious.

Which Kind of Dinosaur Are You?

★ ★

1. Choose a stack of food:

a. Cookies

b. Bacon

c. Waffles

d. Pancakes

2. Choose a snack:

a. Cheese and crackers

b. Mozzarella sticks

c. Popcorn

d. Fruit

3. Choose a character from *The Flintstones*:

a. Wilma Flintstone

b. Fred Flintstone

c. Barney Rubble

d. Betty Rubble

4. Choose a fictional place:

a. Hogwarts

b. Gotham City

c. The Emerald City

d. Neverland

5. Choose a fictional creature:

a. Dragon

b. The Loch Ness monster

c. Pegasus

d. Fairy

6. Choose a superpower you wish you had:

a. Ability to fly

b. Superstrength

c. Mind control

d. Invisibility

7. Choose an animal:

a. Owl

b. Wolf

c. Rhino

d. Giraffe

• •

If you picked mostly As—you got Pterodactyl.

- You're determined, and you don't let anyone hold you down.

If you picked mostly Bs—you got _Tyrannosaurus rex_.

- You're strong and powerful.

If you picked mostly Cs—you got Stegosaurus.

- You're often overlooked, but you're fierce and passionate.

If you picked mostly Ds—you got Brontosaurus.

- You're gentle and caring.

Are You a Good Noodle or Not?

★★

1. Finish the sentence: I love _____.

   a. My family

   b. Money

2. Do you ever volunteer?

   a. Yes

   b. No

3. Would you risk your life for anyone else?

   a. Yes

   b. No

4. Can you remember the last good deed you did?

   a. Yes

   b. No

5. Do you always make your deadlines?

   a. Of course

   b. No

6. Do you like to argue?

   a. Not really

   b. Yes

7. Do you put deep thought into all your loved ones' birthday gifts?

   a. All the time

   b. Not really

8. What's one thing you wish the world had more of?

   a. Peace

   b. Tater tots

9. Last, do you like noodles?

   a. I love them

   b. Nope

● ●

If you picked mostly As—You're a Good Noodle.

If you picked mostly Bs—You're not a Good Noodle.

Which Care Bear Are You?

★★★

1. Choose a candy:

a. Hershey's Kisses Milk Chocolate

b. Skittles

c. Reese's Peanut Butter Cups

d. SweeTarts

e. Jelly Belly jelly beans

f. Sour Patch Kids

2. Choose a flower:

a. Lilac

b. Sunflower

c. Water lily

d. Daffodil

e. Tulip

f. Rose

3. Choose a kids' toy:

a. Playhouse

b. Remote-control car

c. Pogo stick

d. Easy-Bake Oven

e. Nintendo DS

f. Legos

4. Choose some nuts:

a. Walnuts

b. Cashews

c. Pistachios

d. Peanuts

e. Almonds

f. I don't like nuts

5. Choose a song:

a. "Hello" by Adele

b. "Finesse" by Bruno Mars featuring Cardi B

c. "Eye of the Tiger" by Survivor

d. "Birthday" by Katy Perry

e. "Break Free" by Ariana Grande

f. "Bohemian Rhapsody" by Queen

6. Choose a snack:

a. String cheese

b. Glazed doughnut holes

c. Chex Mix

d. Fruit

e. Goldfish crackers

f. Oreos

7. Choose a *SpongeBob SquarePants* character:

a. Sandy Cheeks

b. SpongeBob SquarePants

c. Sheldon J. Plankton

d. Mr. Krabs

e. Patrick Star

f. Squidward Q. Tentacles   *Continued*

If you picked mostly As—you got Harmony Bear.

If you picked mostly Bs—you got Funshine Bear.

If you picked mostly Cs—you got Good Luck Bear.

If you picked mostly Ds—you got Cheer Bear.

If you picked mostly Es—you got Laugh-a-Lot Bear.

If you picked mostly Fs—you got Grumpy Bear.

Which Disney Dog Are You?

✯ ✯ ✯ ✯✯ ✯ ✯ ✯ ✯ ✯ ✯✯ ✯ ✯ ✯ ✯ ✯ ✯ ✯✯ ✯ ✯ ✯ ✯ ✯ ✯✯ ✯ ✯ ✯ ✯ ✯ ✯ ✯✯

1. Choose a cartoon animal:

a. Remy

b. Bugs Bunny

c. Garfield

d. Mickey Mouse

e. Nemo

f. Bambi

2. Choose a ball:

a. Baseball

b. Bowling ball

c. Tennis ball

d. Soccer ball

e. Meatball

f. Volleyball

3. Choose a pop:

a. Sprite

b. Orange Fanta

c. Root beer

d. Pepsi

e. Diet Coke

f. Coca-Cola

Continued

4. Choose an activity:

a. Listening to music

b. Hanging with friends

c. Eating

d. Sleeping

e. Baking/cooking

f. Drawing

5. Choose a place to hang out:

a. The club

b. Your house

c. A lake

d. A park

e. A mall

f. The beach

• •

If you picked mostly As—you got Bolt from *Bolt*.

If you picked mostly Bs—you got Pluto from *Mickey Mouse Clubhouse*.

If you picked mostly Cs—you got Dug from *Up*.

If you picked mostly Ds—you got Pongo from *101 Dalmatians*.

If you picked mostly Es—you got Lady from *Lady and the Tramp*.

If you picked mostly Fs—you got Nana from *Peter Pan*.

Which Fictional Bear Are You?

✫ ✫ ✫ ✫✫ ✫ ✫ ✫ ✫ ✫✫ ✫ ✫ ✫ ✫ ✫✫ ✫ ✫ ✫ ✫ ✫✫ ✫ ✫ ✫ ✫ ✫✫ ✫ ✫ ✫ ✫ ✫✫

1. Pick a wild animal:

a. Hippo

b. Lemur

c. Anteater

d. Buffalo

e. Monkey

2. Pick a food that starts with B:

a. Beans

b. Butter

c. Brownie

d. Beef

e. Bread

3. Pick a hobby:

a. Golf

b. Reading

c. Magic

d. Backpacking

e. Baking

4. Pick a fruit:

a. Blueberries

b. Grapes

c. Raspberries

Continued

d. Banana

e. Apple

5. Pick a color:

a. Green

b. Yellow

c. Pink

d. Purple

e. Red

6. Pick a piece of technology:

a. Flat-screen TV

b. Tablet

c. Smartphone

d. Video camera

e. Smart watch

• •

If you picked mostly As—you got Yogi Bear from *The Yogi Bear Show*.

If you picked mostly Bs—you got Winnie the Pooh from *Winnie the Pooh*.

If you picked mostly Cs—you got Cheer Bear from *The Care Bears*.

If you picked mostly Ds—you got Baloo from *The Jungle Book*.

If you picked mostly Es—you got Paddington Bear from *Paddington*.

Which Pie Flavor Are You?

1. Which of these words describes you best?

   a. Focused

   b. Energetic

   c. Adventurous

   d. Joyful

   e. Generous

   f. Lazy

2. Which of these is your favorite meal?

   a. Dessert time

   b. Snack time

   c. Breakfast

   d. Brunch

   e. Lunch

   f. Dinner

3. Which of these places would you visit?

   a. Copenhagen

   b. Sydney

   c. Paris

   d. New York City

   e. The Maldives

   f. Los Angeles

Continued

4. Which of these is your favorite animal?

a. Koala bear

b. Cheetah

c. Hamster

d. Dog

e. Cat

f. Dolphin

5. Which of these is your favorite ice cream flavor?

a. Pistachio

b. Mint chocolate chip

c. Butter pecan

d. Strawberry

e. Vanilla

f. Chocolate

6. Which of these is your favorite TV show?

a. *Modern Family*

b. *Shameless*

c. *Survivor*

d. *Black-ish*

e. *Friends*

f. *The Walking Dead*

7. Which of these is your favorite fruit?

a. Strawberries

b. Grapes

c. Watermelon

d. Apple

e. Blueberries

f. Banana

• •

If you picked mostly As—you got Key Lime Pie.

• Your loved ones are the key to your happiness.

If you picked mostly Bs—you got Lemon Meringue Pie.

• To you, life is boring without a little zest.

If you picked mostly Cs—you got Pumpkin Pie.

• You love to carve your own adventures. You take the path less traveled.

If you picked mostly Ds—you got Apple Pie.

• You're caring, all the way to your core.

If you picked mostly Es—you got Blueberry Pie.

• You always try to make those around you happy because you hate when people are feeling blue.

If you picked mostly Fs—you got Chocolate Silk Pie.

• Nothing is sweeter to you than being able to have your alone time.

Which Food Mascot Are You?

★ ★

1. Choose a word to describe yourself:

   a. Athletic

   b. Motherly

   c. Energetic

   d. Lazy

   e. Smart

2. Choose a kind of potato:

   a. Baked potato

   b. Cheesy potatoes

   c. French fries

   d. Tater tots

   e. Mashed potatoes

3. Choose a famous athlete:

   a. Michael Phelps

   b. Serena Williams

   c. Kobe Bryant

   d. Tom Brady

   e. Cristiano Ronaldo

4. Choose a word to describe your day so far:

   a. Fine

   b. Busy

   c. Exciting

   d. Boring

   e. Normal

5. Choose a food:

a. Potato chips

b. Pancakes

c. Cereal

d. Cinnamon rolls

e. Almonds

6. Choose a color:

a. Dark blue

b. Orange

c. Red

d. Light blue

e. Dark purple

7. Choose a restaurant:

a. Buffalo Wild Wings

b. Culver's

c. Red Robin

d. The Cheesecake Factory

e. Panera Bread

• •

If you picked mostly As—you got Tony the Tiger from Frosted Flakes cereal.

- You're an active person with lots of grit.

If you picked mostly Bs—you got Mrs. Butterworth from Mrs. Butterworth's syrup.

- You have mom tendencies. You like to take care of others.

Continued

If you picked mostly Cs—you got Tricks, the Trix Rabbit, from Trix cereal.

- Energy is your middle name.

If you picked mostly Ds—you got Poppin' Fresh, the Pillsbury Doughboy, from Pillsbury.

- You're a big ball of joy, but you tend to be lazier than most.

If you picked mostly Es—you got Mr. Peanut from Planters peanuts.

- Your're smart, and you don't reveal much about yourself. You're one tough nut to crack.

Which Two Animals Are You a Mix Of?

1. Choose a holiday:

a. Christmas

b. Halloween

c. New Year's

2. Choose a food:

a. Nachos

b. Pasta

c. Sandwich

3. Choose a pet:

a. Dog

b. Hamster

c. Cat

4. Choose a season:

a. Summer

b. Fall

c. Winter

5. Choose a condiment:

a. Ranch dressing

b. Barbecue sauce

c. Ketchup

Continued

6. Choose a pie flavor:

a. Chocolate

b. Blueberry

c. Cherry

7. Choose a social media platform:

a. YouTube

b. Twitter

c. Snapchat

8. Choose a candy:

a. Skittles

b. Snickers

c. Laffy Taffy

9. Choose a drink:

a. Pop

b. Milk

c. Lemonade

• •

If you picked mostly As—you got Cow and Dog.

• You're very fun and energetic.

If you picked mostly Bs—you got Panda and Cat.

• You're very lazy at times; however, you always stand your ground.

If you picked mostly Cs—you got Whale and Giraffe.

• You have the biggest heart and always stick your neck out for others.

Are You Sliced, Shredded, or Melted Cheese?

★★★ Continued

1. Pick a cheesy dish:

a. Grilled cheese

b. Nachos

c. Macaroni and cheese

2. Pick a holiday:

a. Your birthday

b. Halloween

c. Christmas

3. Pick an athletic clothing brand:

a. Under Armour

b. Nike

c. Adidas

4. Pick a season:

a. Fall

b. Winter

c. Summer

5. Pick a cheesy pickup line:

a. "You must be a banana, because I find you a-peeling."

b. "If you were a booger, I'd pick you first."

c. If you were a vegetable, you'd be a cute-cumber."

Continued

6. Pick a cheesy snack:

a. Cheez-It crackers

b. Cheetos Puffs

c. Cheese popcorn

7. Pick a type of cheese:

a. Colby jack

b. Mozzarella

c. Parmesan

8. Pick a food mascot:

a. Poppin' Fresh, the Pillsbury Doughboy

b. Kool-Aid Man

c. Tony the Tiger

● ●

If you picked mostly As—you got Sliced Cheese.

- You're full of Gouda cheer.

If you picked mostly Bs—you got Melted Cheese.

- You Brie-lieve in always being yourself.

If you picked mostly Cs—you got Shredded Cheese.

- You're grate at bringing the fun to every situation.

Which *Charlie and the Chocolate Factory* Character Are You?

1. Which is your favorite color?

  a. Maroon

  b. Pink

  c. Black

  d. Blue

  e. Green

  f. Red

2. Which is your favorite TV show?

  a. *Full House*

  b. *Gossip Girl*

  c. *The Walking Dead*

  d. *Friends*

  e. *The Office*

  f. *Bob's Burgers*

3. Which of these is your favorite Disney Channel show?

  a. *Girl Meets World*

  b. *Hannah Montana*

  c. *The Suite Life of Zack & Cody*

  d. *That's So Raven*

  e. *Jessie*

  f. *Austin & Ally*

Continued

4. Which of these is your favorite song?

a. "Halo" by Beyoncé

b. "Thriller" by Michael Jackson

c. "Too Good at Goodbyes" by Sam Smith

d. "It Wasn't Me" by Shaggy

e. "What Do You Mean?" by Justin Bieber

f. "Humble" by Kendrick Lamar

5. Which of these words describes you best?

a. Caring

b. Opinionated

c. Sarcastic

d. Competitive

e. Lazy

f. Funny

6. Which of these foods is the tastiest?

a. Chicken tenders

b. Sushi

c. Pizza

d. Pasta

e. Tacos

f. Ice cream

7. Which of these is your favorite candy?

a. M&M's

b. Sour Patch Kids

c. Airheads

d. Hershey's Kisses Milk Chocolate

e. Butterfinger bar

f. Skittles

8. Which of these is your least favorite candy?

a. Sour Patch Kids

b. Skittles

c. Hershey's Kisses Milk Chocolate

d. Butterfinger bar

e. Airheads

f. M&M's

● ●

If you picked mostly As—you got Charlie Bucket.

If you picked mostly Bs—you got Veruca Salt.

If you picked mostly Cs—you got Mike Teavee.

If you picked mostly Ds—you got Violet Beauregarde.

If you picked mostly Es—you got Augustus Gloop.

If you picked mostly Fs—you got Willy Wonka.

Which Kind of Bird Are You?

★ ★

1. Choose a country:

a. Italy

b. Australia

c. Brazil

d. United States

e. England

2. Choose a bread:

a. Crescent roll

b. Banana bread

c. Corn bread

d. Baguette

e. Bagel

3. Choose a music genre:

a. Classical

b. Pop

c. Rock

d. Country

e. Rap

4. Choose a brand:

a. Facebook

b. Google

c. Disney

d. Apple

e. Coca-Cola

5. Choose a cartoon character:

a. Tweety Bird

b. Scooby-Doo

c. Marge Simpson

d. Kim Possible

e. Patrick Star

6. Choose a cereal:

a. Cheerios

b. Froot Loops

c. Lucky Charms

d. Frosted Flakes

e. Cap'n Crunch

7. Choose a word to describe yourself:

a. Elegant

b. Cheerful

c. Loyal

d. Courageous

e. Funny

8. Choose something that flies:

a. Butterfly

b. Time

c. Plane

d. Rocket

e. Bat

Continued

● ●

If you picked mostly As—you got Dove.

• You're peaceful and enjoy the company of others.

If you picked mostly Bs—you got Flamingo.

• You're outgoing.

If you picked mostly Cs—you got Parrot.

• You're bright and very curious.

If you picked mostly Ds—you got Eagle.

• You're strong and persistent.

If you picked mostly Es—you got Pigeon.

• You're crazy.

Are You Rock, Paper, or Scissors?

★ ★

1. Choose a potato dish:

a. Waffle fries

b. Tater tots

c. Potato wedges

2. Choose a Powerpuff Girl:

a. Bubbles

b. Blossom

c. Buttercup

3. Choose a candy:

a. Airheads

b. Nerds

c. Kit Kat

4. Choose a chipmunk from *Alvin and the Chipmunks*:

a. Simon

b. Theodore

c. Alvin

5. Choose a Disney sidekick:

a. Baymax

b. Flounder

c. Mushu

Continued

6. Choose a primary color:

a. Yellow

b. Blue

c. Red

7. Choose a pizza topping:

a. Onions

b. Sausage

c. Pepperoni

8. Choose an iconic trio:

a. Destiny's Child

b. The Three Stooges

c. Harry, Ron, and Hermione

9. Choose a food combination:

a. Bacon and eggs

b. Grilled cheese and tomato soup

c. Peanut butter and jelly

10. Choose a mythical creature:

a. Fairy

b. Mermaid

c. Unicorn

11. Choose a Neapolitan ice cream flavor:

a. Vanilla

b. Chocolate

c. Strawberry

12. Choose a triangle-shaped food:

a. Watermelon slice

b. Pizza slice

c. Tortilla chip

• •

If you picked mostly As—you got Paper.

• You're delicate and simple.

If you picked mostly Bs—you got Rock.

• You're strong and stubborn.

If you picked mostly Cs—you got Scissors.

• You're sharp and hard to please.

Which Justin Bieber Song Are You?

1. Pick a snack:

a. Cereal

b. Pretzels

c. Yogurt

d. Potato chips

2. Pick a social media platform:

a. Facebook

b. Twitter

c. YouTube

d. Pinterest

3. Pick a candy that starts with J:

a. Jujubes

b. Jolly Ranchers

c. Jelly Belly jelly beans

d. Junior Mints

4. Pick a season:

a. Summer

b. Fall

c. Spring

d. Winter

5. Pick a Canadian city:

a. Toronto

b. Montreal

c. Calgary

d. Vancouver

6. Pick a singer to see live in concert:

a. Travis Scott

b. Ariana Grande

c. Justin Bieber

d. Post Malone

7. Pick a sport:

a. Basketball

b. Baseball

c. Soccer

d. Football

8. Pick a word to describe yourself:

a. Bold

b. Pretty

c. Sensitive

d. Crazy

• •

If you picked mostly As—you got "Confident."

If you picked mostly Bs—you got "Beauty and a Beat."

If you picked mostly Cs—you got "Baby."

If you picked mostly Ds—you got "No Sense."

Which Gross Food Are You?

1. Choose some beans:

    a. Baked beans

    b. Green beans

    c. Jelly beans

2. Choose a holiday:

    a. Your birthday

    b. Thanksgiving

    c. Christmas

3. Choose a mammal:

    a. Otter

    b. Rhino

    c. Squirrel

4. Choose a drink:

    a. Milkshake

    b. Smoothie

    c. Slushie

5. Choose a movie character:

    a. Harry Potter

    b. Jack Sparrow

    c. Luke Skywalker

6. Choose a snack brand:

a. Doritos

b. Popchips

c. Wheat Thins

7. Choose a job:

a. Teacher

b. Hairstylist

c. Interior designer

• •

If you picked mostly As—you got Baked Bean Pizza.

• You're saucy and unique.

If you picked mostly Bs—you got Spam.

• You're contained and laid back.

If you picked mostly Cs—you got Soggy Bread.

• You're soft and sweet.

Which Type of Berry Are You?

★ ★★ ★★ ★ ★★★ ★★ ★ ★ ★★ ★★ ★★ ★★★ ★★ ★ ★ ★★ ★★ ★★★ ★★ ★ ★ ★★ ★★ ★★ ★★ ★★ ★★ ★

1. Choose a word to describe yourself:

a. Innocent

b. Calming

c. Weird

d. Moody

2. Choose a social media platform:

a. Snapchat

b. Facebook

c. YouTube

d. Twitter

3. Choose an appetizer:

a. Bread

b. Salad

c. Quesadilla

d. Buffalo wings

4. Choose a vegetable:

a. Carrot

b. Peas

c. Corn

d. Onion

5. Choose a fruity dessert:

a. Strawberry shortcake

b. Fruit Popsicle

c. Apple pie

d. Key lime pie

6. Choose a movie genre:

a. Family-friendly

b. Comedy

c. Action

d. Suspense

7. Choose an arctic animal:

a. Penguin

b. Walrus

c. Polar bear

d. Killer whale

8. What is your zodiac sign?

a. Gemini, Libra, or Aquarius

b. Taurus, Virgo, or Capricorn

c. Cancer, Scorpio, or Pisces

d. Aries, Leo, or Sagittarius

• •

If you picked mostly As—you got Strawberry.

- You have great manners, and you're always polite.

If you picked mostly Bs—you got Blueberry.

- Your sense of humor is one of your strongest traits.

If you picked mostly Cs—you got Raspberry.

- You're persistent and a bit of a daredevil.

If you picked mostly Ds—you got Blackberry.

- You're hard on the outside but full of love on the inside.

Which Cat Breed Are You?

1. Choose a country:

a. England

b. China

c. Australia

d. Egypt

2. Choose a flower:

a. Hydrangea

b. Rose

c. Sunflower

d. Tulip

3. Choose a TV show:

a. *Modern Family*

b. *Fuller House*

c. *Brooklyn Nine-Nine*

d. *The Walking Dead*

4. Choose an activity:

a. Napping

b. Painting

c. Dancing

d. Eating

5. Choose a milk:

a. Almond milk

b. 1% milk

c. Chocolate milk

d. Soy milk

6. Choose a meat:

a. Turkey

b. Ham

c. Chicken

d. Salami

7. Choose a seasoning:

a. Cajun

b. Salt

c. Italian herb

d. Garlic pepper

8. Choose a dog breed:

a. Australian shepherd

b. Poodle

c. Beagle

d. Pug

9. Choose a cat pun:

a. Looking good, feline good

b. Life is purr-fect

c. Stay pawsitive

d. You've got to be kitten me

Continued

• •

If you picked mostly As—you got Russian Blue Cat.

- You're practical.

If you picked mostly Bs—you got Persian Cat.

- You're elegant.

If you picked mostly Cs—you got Siamese Cat.

- You're hilarious.

If you picked mostly Ds—you got Sphynx Cat.

- You're entertaining.

Are You More like Luke Skywalker, Princess Leia, or Han Solo from *Star Wars?*

★ ★

1. Pick a slushie flavor:
a. Blue raspberry

b. Cherry

c. Coca-Cola

2. Pick an item of jewelry:
a. Bracelet

b. Necklace

c. Ring

3. Do you prefer hard or soft taco shells?
a. Hard shells

b. Soft shells

c. I don't like tacos

4. Do you prefer rock, paper, or scissors?
a. Rock

b. Paper

c. Scissors

5. Pick an animal:
a. Giraffe

b. Zebra

c. Lion

Continued

297

6. Pick a pasta:

a. Macaroni and cheese

b. Fettuccine Alfredo

c. Chicken Parmesan

7. Pick a way to spend your Friday night:

a. Playing laser tag

b. Going to a movie

c. Staying in and watching Netflix

8. Which is your favorite singer?

a. Eminem

b. Sia

c. David Bowie

9. Are you in a relationship at the moment?

a. No

b. It's complicated

c. Yes

10. Where would you like to go on vacation?

a. On a Caribbean cruise

b. To a resort in Hawaii

c. To Paris

• •

If you picked mostly As—you got Luke Skywalker.

If you picked mostly Bs—you got Princess Leia.

If you picked mostly Cs—you got Han Solo.

Which Flavor of Popcorn Are You?

1. Choose an instrument you'd love to learn how to play:

  a. Drums

  b. Guitar

  c. Piano

  d. Violin

  e. Banjo

2. Choose a *SpongeBob SquarePants* character:

  a. Patrick Star

  b. Mr. Krabs

  c. Squidward Q. Tentacles

  d. Sandy Cheeks

  e. SpongeBob SquarePants

3. Choose a type of bagel:

  a. Asiago cheese

  b. Chocolate chip

  c. Plain

  d. Poppy seed

  e. Cinnamon

4. Choose an American food:

  a. Nachos

  b. Potato chips

Continued

c. Hot dog

d. Chicken and waffles

e. Tater tots

5. Which is the most annoying?

a. When people copy you

b. Slow walkers

c. When people chew with their mouths open

d. Bad grammar

e. When people don't flush

6. Choose a Disney animated movie:

a. *Zootopia*

b. *Peter Pan*

c. *Beauty and the Beast*

d. *101 Dalmatians*

e. *The Lion King*

7. Choose a fruit:

a. Banana

b. Apple

c. Watermelon

d. Pineapple

e. Strawberries

8. Choose a corn-based dish:

a. Cheesy corn

b. Corn chowder

c. Corn bread

d. Corn casserole

e. Corn dip

● ●

If you picked mostly As—you got Cheese Popcorn.

• You're cheesy and loud.

If you picked mostly Bs—you got Buttered Popcorn.

• You're forgetful but determined.

If you picked mostly Cs—you got Kettle Corn.

• You're particular and adventurous.

If you picked mostly Ds—you got White Cheddar Popcorn.

• You're thoughtful and sharp.

If you picked mostly Es—you got Tutti-Frutti Popcorn.

• You're fruity and fun.

Which Kind of Bear Are You?

1. Choose a pattern:

  a. Stripes

  b. Chevron

  c. Polka dots

  d. Checks

2. Choose a candy:

  a. Milk Duds

  b. Swedish Fish

  c. Twizzlers

  d. Milky Way

3. Choose a Netflix TV show:

  a. *Stranger Things*

  b. *Orange Is the New Black*

  c. *On My Block*

  d. *One Day at a Time*

4. Choose a meat:

  a. Steak

  b. Salmon

  c. Chicken

  d. I don't like meat

5. Choose a word to describe yourself:

  a. Loyal

  b. Hardworking

c. Weird

d. Lazy

6. Choose a cake flavor:

a. Chocolate

b. Vanilla

c. Red velvet

d. Strawberry

7. Choose a junk food:

a. Pizza

b. Doughnut

c. Cheese fries

d. Oreo

8. Choose a cartoon animal:

a. Donald Duck from *Mickey Mouse Clubhouse*

b. Tom from *Tom and Jerry*

c. Blue from *Blue's Clues*

d. Garfield from *Garfield*

• •

If you picked mostly As—you got Black Bear.

• In one word: you're strong.

If you picked mostly Bs—you got Polar Bear.

• In one word: you're fearful.

If you picked mostly Cs—you got Sloth Bear.

• In one word: you're unique.

If you picked mostly Ds—you got Panda Bear.

• In one word: you're gentle.

Which Kind of Sandwich Are You?

★ ★

1. Choose a social media platform:

- a. Instagram
- b. Twitter
- c. YouTube
- d. Facebook
- e. Snapchat

2. Choose some chips:

- a. Lay's Classic
- b. Garden Salsa SunChips
- c. Cheetos Puffs
- d. Pringles Sour Cream & Onion
- e. Chocolate chips

3. Choose a milkshake flavor:

- a. Cookies and cream
- b. Strawberry
- c. Orange cream
- d. Caramel
- e. S'mores

4. Choose a city:

- a. Chicago
- b. Los Angeles
- c. Dallas

d. St. Louis

e. Ft. Lauderdale

5. Choose a vowel:

a. A

b. U

c. E

d. O

e. I

6. Choose a flavor of Skittles:

a. Original

b. Wild Berry

c. Tropical

d. Sweets & Sours

e. Sour

• •

If you picked mostly As—you got Peanut Butter Sandwich.

• You enjoy the classic things in life.

If you picked mostly Bs—you got Breakfast Sandwich.

• You like to step out of your comfort zone.

If you picked mostly Cs—you got Grilled Cheese Sandwich.

• You're humorous and predictable.

If you picked mostly Ds—you got Meatball Sub.

• You always stand out in a crowd.

If you picked mostly Es—you got Ice Cream Sandwich.

• You're a sweetheart with a big sweet tooth.

Which Kind of Frog Are You?

1. Pick a snack:

   a. Granola bar

   b. Candy

   c. Crunchy Flamin' Hot Cheetos

2. Pick a celebrity to be friends with:

   a. Ellen DeGeneres

   b. Jennifer Lawrence

   c. Cardi B

3. Which of the following is the most annoying?

   a. Being ignored

   b. Slow drivers

   c. When people stand too close

4. Pick a game to play:

   a. Uno

   b. The Game of Life

   c. Blackjack

5. Pick a movie genre:

   a. Romance

   b. Comedy

   c. Suspense

6. Pick an animal that hops:

a. Rabbit

b. Kangaroo

c. Jumping spider

7. What is your favorite time of day?

a. Morning

b. Afternoon

c. Night

● ●

If you picked mostly As—you got Glass Frog.

- You're giddy and very open when it comes to your feelings and thoughts.

If you picked mostly Bs—you got Tree Frog.

- You don't like to stand out; you prefer being one of many in a crowd.

If you picked mostly Cs—you got Poison Dart Frog.

- You aren't one to stand down from a fight. You share your opinion, no matter what.

Which Kind of Popsicle Are You?

★ ★

1. Pick a season:

  a. Summer

  b. Winter

  c. Spring

  d. Fall

2. Pick a summer activity:

  a. Swimming

  b. Camping

  c. Tanning

  d. Tubing

3. Pick a fall activity:

  a. Carving pumpkins

  b. Watching scary movies

  c. Picking apples

  d. Going on a hayride

4. Pick a winter activity:

  a. Sledding

  b. Drinking hot cocoa

  c. Ice skating

  d. Snowboarding

5. Pick a spring activity:

  a. Bike riding

  b. Picnicking

c. Picking flowers

d. Walking through the park

6. Pick a candy flavor:

a. Blue raspberry

b. Chocolate

c. Cherry

d. Orange

7. Pick a dessert:

a. Rice Krispies Treats

b. Chocolate lava cake

c. Strawberry sundae

d. Orange poke cake

• •

If you picked mostly As—you got Ice Pop.

- You're all about tradition and sticking to what you know.

If you picked mostly Bs—you got Fudge Popsicle.

- You know how to make the best of everything and every situation.

If you picked mostly Cs—you got Fruit Popsicle.

- Everyone thinks you're the sweetest person alive.

If you picked mostly Ds—you got Creamsicle.

- People think they have you figured out, but what's on the inside is a whole different story from what people see.

Which Color of the Rainbow Are You?

★★

1. What really annoys you?

a. Boring people

b. Being pressured

c. Being ignored

d. Fighting

e. Being looked down on

f. Haters

2. Who is your favorite female celebrity?

a. Miley Cyrus

b. Reese Witherspoon

c. Emma Watson

d. Angelina Jolie

e. Kim Kardashian

f. Ellen DeGeneres

3. If you had to bake something, what would you make?

a. A layer cake to decorate

b. Strawberry cheesecake

c. M&M's cookies

d. Macarons

e. Butterscotch brownies

f. Red velvet cupcakes

4. What would you consider for a New Year's resolution?

a. Work more on your studies

b. Get fit

c. Meet a new person each day

d. Stop prejudging others

e. Get a promotion

f. Make a move on your crush

5. Which kind of vacation sounds most appealing?

a. Taking a road trip across the United States

b. Hanging around Los Angeles

c. Going on a family cruise

d. Camping at a national park

e. Exploring Paris

f. Staying at a beach resort

6. What clique were you part of in high school?

a. The art crew

b. The athletes

c. The smarties

d. The quiet kids

e. The popular crowd

f. I wasn't in a clique

7. Which food smells the best?

a. Pie

b. Popcorn

c. Barbecued meat

d. Freshly baked bread

e. Coffee

f. Freshly baked cookies

Continued

• •

If you picked mostly As—you got Orange.

   • You're all about creativity.

If you picked mostly Bs—you got Yellow.

   • You're all about optimism and cheer.

If you picked mostly Cs—you got Green.

   • You're all about harmony and relationships.

If you picked mostly Ds—you got Blue.

   • You're all about peace and tranquility.

If you picked mostly Es—you got Purple.

   • You're all about sophistication and power.

If you picked mostly Fs—you got Red.

   • You're all about love.

Which Kind of Rabbit Are You?

* * * ** * * * * * ** * * * * ** * * * * ** * * * * ** * * **

1. Pick something you can't live without:

   a. Naps

   b. Dogs

   c. Family

   d. Pizza

2. Pick a finger food:

   a. Cheese and crackers

   b. Breadsticks

   c. Cucumber bites

   d. Mozzarella sticks

3. Pick a place to live:

   a. In the city

   b. In the country

   c. On a lake

   d. On the beach

4. Pick a vegetable:

   a. Celery

   b. Carrot

   c. Peas

   d. Corn

Continued

313

5. Pick a hobby:

a. Sports

b. Painting

c. Photography

d. Sleeping

6. Pick a breakfast food:

a. Waffles

b. Pancakes

c. French toast

d. Cinnamon roll

7. Pick a pet peeve:

a. Being ignored

b. When people don't flush

c. Loud chewers

d. Slow drivers

8. Pick something to read:

a. A magazine

b. A book

c. Your social media

d. A menu

9. Pick an Easter candy:

a. Chocolate bunny

b. Jelly beans

c. Cadbury Creme Egg

d. Marshmallow Peeps

• •

If you picked mostly As—you got Checkered Giant Rabbit.

> • In one word: you're emotional.

If you picked mostly Bs—you got Eastern Cottontail Rabbit.

> • In one word: you're thoughtful.

If you picked mostly Cs—you got Holland Lop Rabbit.

> • In one word: you're conscientious.

If you picked mostly Ds—you got Giant Chinchilla Rabbit.

> • In one word: you're irritable.

Which Fictional Fish Are You?

★ ★

1. Pick an animal movie:

   a. *101 Dalmatians*

   b. *Marley & Me*

   c. *Ratatouille*

2. Pick a kind of potato:

   a. Potato chips

   b. Mashed potatoes

   c. French fries

3. Pick a school subject:

   a. History

   b. Science

   c. English

4. Pick a holiday:

   a. Christmas

   b. Thanksgiving

   c. Halloween

5. Pick a candy:

   a. Skittles

   b. Twizzlers

   c. Reese's Peanut Butter Cups

6. Pick a social media platform:

   a. Instagram

   b. Facebook

   c. Twitter

7. Pick a color:

   a. Yellow

   b. Red

   c. Blue

8. Pick the most embarrassing thing:

   a. Falling in public

   b. Failing at a job

   c. Walking in on someone in the bathroom

● ●

If you picked mostly As—you got Flounder from *The Little Mermaid*.

If you picked mostly Bs—you got Mrs. Poppy Puff from *SpongeBob SquarePants*.

If you picked mostly Cs—you got Dory from *Finding Nemo*.

Which Kind of Goat Are You?

★★★

1. Pick a class in school:

   a. English

   b. Science

   c. History

   d. Gym

2. Pick a sports movie:

   a. *DodgeBall: A True Underdog Story*

   b. *The Blind Side*

   c. *Air Bud*

   d. *Remember the Titans*

3. Pick a color:

   a. Orange

   b. Purple

   c. Green

   d. Blue

4. Pick a Wonder of the World to visit:

   a. Great Wall of China

   b. Machu Picchu

   c. Roman Colosseum

   d. Taj Mahal

5. Pick a farm animal:

   a. Chicken

   b. Horse

c. Pig

d. Cow

6. Pick a vegetable:

a. Corn

b. Broccoli

c. Green beans

d. Peas

7. Pick a flower:

a. Lily

b. Rose

c. Tulip

d. Daisy

• •

If you picked mostly As—you got Alpine Goat.

- You have a great sense of humor, and your comedic timing is stellar.

If you picked mostly Bs—you got Angora Goat.

- You're very aware of your surroundings. You never back down from a fight, and you're loyal as can be.

If you picked mostly Cs—you got Saanen Goat.

- You have a laid-back personality, and you never let little things bother you.

If you picked mostly Ds—you got Boer Goat.

- You're extremely passionate when it comes to the things you love.

Which *Wizard of Oz* Character Are You?

1. Choose a classic movie:

   a. *Miracle on 34th Street*

   b. *Singin' in the Rain*

   c. *Fantasia*

   d. *Mary Poppins*

2. Choose a Disney sidekick:

   a. Piglet from *Winnie the Pooh*

   b. Baloo from *The Jungle Book*

   c. Olaf from *Frozen*

   d. Gus from *Cinderella*

3. Choose a type of shoe:

   a. Slides

   b. High heels

   c. Boots

   d. Sneakers

4. If you were a princess, what color would you want your gown to be?

   a. Gold

   b. Blue

   c. Silver

   d. Emerald

5. Choose a word to describe yourself:

a. Timid

b. Brave

c. Unique

d. Logical

6. Choose a type of cuisine:

a. Indian

b. French

c. Chinese

d. Mexican

7. Choose a line from *The Wizard of Oz*:

a. "Lions and tigers and bears, oh my!"

b. "I've a feeling we're not in Kansas anymore."

c. "I'll get you, my pretty, and your little dog, too!"

d. "There's no place like home."

• •

If you picked mostly As—you got the Cowardly Lion.

If you picked mostly Bs—you got Dorothy.

If you picked mostly Cs—you got the Tin Man.

If you picked mostly Ds—you got the Scarecrow.

Which Famous Spy Are You?

1. **If you could shape-shift into one of these mythical creatures, which would you choose?**

   a. Fairy

   b. Unicorn

   c. Werewolf

   d. Yeti

   e. Mermaid

2. **Choose a Disney character to be your sidekick:**

   a. Princess Merida from *Brave*

   b. Chicken Little from *Chicken Little*

   c. Basil from *The Great Mouse Detective*

   d. Mushu from *Mulan*

   e. Mike Wazowski from *Monsters, Inc.*

3. **Choose a school subject to get rid of forever:**

   a. Physics

   b. Writing

   c. Calculus

   d. Phys ed

   e. History

4. **Choose a spy gadget:**

   a. Spyglass

   b. Listening device

   c. Tracking device

  d. Camera pen

  e. Remote-controlled robot

5. Choose a strong female character:

  a. Beatrix Kiddo from *The Bride*

  b. Storm from Marvel Comics

  c. Wonder Woman from *Wonder Woman*

  d. Rey from *Star Wars*

  e. Katniss Everdeen from *The Hunger Games*

6. Choose a crunchy food:

  a. Granola

  b. Cereal

  c. Carrot

  d. Pretzels

  e. Potato chips

• •

If you picked mostly **As**—you got **Clover** from *Totally Spies!*

If you picked mostly **Bs**—you got **Austin Powers** from *Austin Powers: International Man of Mystery*.

If you picked mostly **Cs**—you got **James Bond** from *Spectre*.

If you picked mostly **Ds**—you got **Bob Ho** from *The Spy Next Door*.

If you picked mostly **Es**—you got **Juni Cortez** from *Spy Kids*.

Which Part of a S'more Are You?

1. What's your opinion of s'mores?

   a. They're delicious

   b. I've never had one

   c. They're okay

2. What's your favorite candy bar?

   a. Hershey's Bar

   b. PayDay

   c. Twix

3. Choose an unconventional sandwich:

   a. Chocolate chip cookie dough ice cream sandwich

   b. Ramen burger

   c. Doughnut breakfast sandwich

4. Which of these places would you want to be your house?

   a. Museum of Ice Cream in San Francisco

   b. TCL Chinese Theatre in Los Angeles

   c. Rainforest Cafe in Chicago

5. Which food-based job would you want to have?

   a. Bakery owner

   b. Chef at a five-star restaurant

   c. Food taste tester

6. **Choose an object to use as a stick to roast your marshmallow:**

   a. Golf club

   b. Cane

   c. Plastic lightsaber

7. **Choose a place to eat a s'more:**

   a. In bed

   b. At work

   c. By a campfire

• •

If you picked mostly As—you got the Chocolate.

   • You're incredibly sweet and love to have fun.

If you picked mostly Bs—you got the Graham Cracker.

   • You're practical and love stability.

If you picked mostly Cs—you got the Marshmallow.

   • You may be a child at heart, but you're the glue that holds everyone together.

Which Part of Lasagna Are You?

1. Which Italian city would you want to live in?

   a. Rome

   b. Milan

   c. Florence

2. Which is your favorite pasta dish ?

   a. Fettuccine Alfredo

   b. Macaroni and cheese

   c. Spaghetti and meatballs

3. Which is your favorite pasta sauce?

   a. Pesto

   b. Five cheese

   c. Marinara

4. Which is your favorite kind of cheese?

   a. Cream cheese

   b. Mozzarella

   c. Cheddar

5. Choose an Italian food:

   a. Antipasto

   b. Calzone

   c. Minestrone

6. Choose a kind of food other than Italian:

a. Chinese

b. American

c. Mexican

7. Which is your favorite part of a pizza?

a. The crust

b. The cheese

c. The toppings

8. Choose a word to describe yourself:

a. Solid

b. Corny

c. Feisty

9. Choose a side to have with pasta:

a. Salad

b. Garlic bread

c. Vegetables

• •

If you picked mostly As—you got the Noodles.

- You're a strong-willed person who always does what's best for yourself.

If you picked mostly Bs—you got the Cheese.

- You're an energetic, sarcastic person.

If you picked mostly Cs—you got the Sauce.

- You stand your ground, and people have learned not to mess with you.

Which Jewel Matches Your Personality?

★ ★

1. Choose a type of pop:

- a. Lemon-lime
- b. Cola
- c. Orange

2. Choose a dog breed:

- a. Corgi
- b. Poodle
- c. Bulldog

3. Choose a type of bagel:

- a. Plain
- b. Whole wheat
- c. Sesame seed

4. Choose a piece of jewelry:

- a. Necklace
- b. Earring
- c. Bracelet

5. Choose something you can't live without:

- a. Makeup
- b. Tea or coffee
- c. Fast food

6. Choose a language:

a. English

b. French

c. Spanish

7. Choose a coffee place:

a. Starbucks

b. Tim Hortons

c. Dunkin' Donuts

8. Choose a European city:

a. Rome

b. Paris

c. London

• •

If you picked mostly As—you got Emerald.

If you picked mostly Bs—you got Sapphire.

If you picked mostly Cs—you got Opal.

Which Insurance Mascot Are You?

★ ★

1. What's something you love?

   a. Being popular

   b. Animals

   c. Traveling

2. How good are you with your money?

   a. Bad

   b. Pretty good

   c. Great

3. How much TV do you watch?

   a. Not much

   b. Average amount

   c. Lots and lots

4. Do you prefer pancakes, waffles, or French toast?

   a. Pancakes

   b. Waffles

   c. French toast

5. Do you prefer white, black, or gray?

   a. White

   b. Black

   c. Gray

6. Do you prefer tennis, badminton, or Ping-Pong?

a. Tennis

b. Badminton

c. Ping-Pong

7. What are your thoughts about social media?

a. I'm obsessed with it

b. It's okay

c. I'm not a big fan of it

8. Do you believe there is life on other planets?

a. Yes

b. No

c. I'm not quite sure

● ●

If you picked mostly As—you got Flo from Progressive.

If you picked mostly Bs—you got the Aflac Duck.

If you picked mostly Cs—you got the GEICO Gecko.

Are You Regular, Chocolate, or Strawberry Milk?

1. Rock, paper, or scissors?

a. Rock

b. Paper

c. Scissors

2. How confident are you?

a. Very confident

b. Somewhat confident

c. Not confident

3. Choose a primary color:

a. Blue

b. Yellow

c. Red

4. Choose something that comes in threes:

a. Three-ring circus

b. Three Wise Men

c. Three Musketeers

5. Which do you find most underrated?

a. The city at night

b. The smell of laundry

c. Tight hugs

6. Which type of people do you dislike the most?

a. Boring people

b. Ignorant people

c. Loud people

7. What excites you?

a. Winning

b. Lazy days

c. Being shown you're appreciated

8. Choose a flavor of lemonade:

a. Strawberry

b. Regular

c. Raspberry

• •

If you picked mostly As—you got Chocolate Milk.

• You're an energetic soul.

If you picked mostly Bs—you got Regular Milk.

• You're the OG.

If you picked mostly Cs—you got Strawberry Milk.

• You're sweeter than most.

Which Kind of Dip Are You?

★★★★★★★★★★★★★★★★★★★★★★★★★★★★★★★★★★★★★★★

1. What is your favorite part of pizza?

a. The toppings

b. The sauce

c. The cheese

d. The crust

2. Choose a food to dip:

a. Tortilla chips

b. French toast sticks

c. Mozzarella sticks

d. Veggies

3. Which of these things do you find most overrated?

a. Apple products

b. Tanning

c. Coffee

d. Pizza

4. What muffin flavor do you find the nastiest?

a. Chocolate chip

b. Zucchini apple

c. Whole wheat blueberry

d. Banana

5. Choose a word to describe your style:

a. Vintage

b. Unique

c. Casual

d. Classy

6. Choose a food-and-drink combination:

a. Milk and cookies

b. Burgers and milkshake

c. Doughnuts and coffee

d. Marshmallows and hot chocolate

7. How do you feel about double-dipping?

a. It doesn't really bother me

b. It's perfectly fine

c. It's disgusting

d. It depends who does it

• •

If you picked mostly As—you got Guacamole.

- You're someone people feel they can turn to when they need help, and you enjoy feeling appreciated.

If you picked mostly Bs—you got Fun Dip.

- You're a crazy ball of energy. Everyone knows you can turn anything into a good time.

If you picked mostly Cs—you got Cheese Fondue.

- You're pretty average, but that doesn't stop you from having a good time with people you're close to.

If you picked mostly Ds—you got Spinach Artichoke Dip.

- You're more sophisticated, and you dislike putting off things until the last minute.

Which Disney Princess and Cartoon Character Are You a Combination Of?

✮✮✮✮✮✮✮✮✮✮✮✮✮✮✮✮✮✮✮✮✮✮✮✮✮✮✮✮✮✮✮✮✮✮✮✮✮✮

1. If you had to be stuck on an island with one of these Disney villains, which would you choose?

   a. Randall Boggs from *Monsters, Inc.*

   b. Captain Hook from *Peter Pan*

   c. Kylo Ren from *Star Wars: The Force Awakens*

   d. Yzma from *The Emperor's New Groove*

2. Which of these color combinations do you like the best?

   a. Red and blue

   b. Orange and purple

   c. White and green

   d. Yellow and turquoise

3. If you could star in a movie, which genre would you want it to be?

   a. Musical

   b. Adventure

   c. Mystery

   d. Comedy

4. How would your friends describe you?

   a. Determined

   b. Selfless

   c. Impulsive

   d. Smart

5. Which party theme seems most fun to you?

a. Hollywood

b. Mardi Gras

c. Hawaiian

d. Costume

6. Which Disney movie series is your favorite?

a. *High School Musical*

b. *Toy Story*

c. *Cars*

d. *The Incredibles*

7. If you could tame a wild animal to be your sidekick, which animal would you choose?

a. Dolphin

b. Monkey

c. Snow leopard

d. Raccoon

8. Which of these things are you most passionate about?

a. Your hobbies

b. Helping others

c. Naps

d. Adventure

9. Choose something you're bad at:

a. Following the rules

b. Letting other people be in charge

c. Listening

d. Staying focused

Continued

● ●

If you picked mostly As—you got Ariel from *The Little Mermaid* **and Squidward Q. Tentacles from** *SpongeBob SquarePants***.**

- You never let anyone keep you from accomplishing your goals. You're passionate about your hobbies, and you don't like anyone telling you what to do.

If you picked mostly Bs—you got Pocahontas from *Pocahontas* **and Dora from** *Dora the Explorer***.**

- You're very selfless and strong-willed. You're someone who normally takes charge.

If you picked mostly Cs—you got Elsa from *Frozen* **and Garfield from** *Garfield: The Movie***.**

- You're stubborn at times and definitely enjoy your alone time, but you're very appreciative of your loved ones.

If you picked mostly Ds—you got Cinderella from *Cinderella* **and Velma Dinkley from** *Scooby-Doo, Where Are You!*

- You always seem to be overlooked, but you never let that stop you from being who you are.

ABOUT THE AUTHOR

Rachel McMahon is a college student at
Grand Valley State University in Michigan.
She began writing quizzes for BuzzFeed in
April 2017, quickly becoming one of the site's
highest-traffic-driving members worldwide. She
lives in a small town just outside Grand Rapids.